QUARTERBACK YOUR INVESTMENT PLAN

THE BASICS FOR BEGINNERS

BY: EAMONN "ED" NOHILLY

First Edition

Personal Finance Publishing
Riverside, California

QUARTERBACK YOUR INVESTMENT PLAN:

THE BASICS FOR BEGINNERS

Eamonn "Ed" Nohilly

Published By: PERSONAL FINANCE PUBLISHING
P.O. Box 55130
Riverside, California 92517

This publication is designed to provide accurate and authoritative information in regard to the subject matter covered. It is sold with the understanding that the publication is not rendering legal, accounting, or other professional service. If legal or other expert assistance is required, the services of a competent professional person should be sought. From a declaration of principles jointly adopted by a committee of the American Bar Association and a Committee of Publishers.

Copyright ©2002 by Eamonn Nohilly
Printed in the United States of America
First Printing 2002
Edited by Melody Girard of Quinn's Word for Word
Cover Design by Lightbourne

Publisher's Cataloging-in-Publication
(Provided by Quality Books, Inc.)

Nohilly, Eamonn.
   Quarterback your investment plan : the basics
for beginners / Eamonn Nohilly. – 1st ed.
   p. cm.
   Includes bibliographical references and index.
   LCCN: 00-91232
   ISBN: 0-9676249-9-1

   1. Investments. 2. Finance, Personal.
1. I. Title

   HG4521.N64 2001   332.6
   QBI00-500118

DEDICATION

To my wife Gemma and our daughters Terriann and Fiona.

May Terriann and Fiona be a part of the first generation of Americans ever to have the opportunity to learn the basics about investing and personal finance during their schooling years.

ACKNOWLEDGEMENTS

My thanks to the many authors whose books I have read that helped me to understand the basics and more about investing. Many of these authors are recommended for your more in-depth reading on specific investment players and also about the economy. These authors have been of invaluable help crystallizing in my mind how I should present the information so that beginners can clearly understand the basics of investing and also the fundamentals about the major investment players. In particular, I want to recognize the indispensable help of the following authors: John Bogle of *Bogle on Mutual Funds* and founder of Vanguard Investment Company; Peter Lynch with John Rothchild of *One Up On Wall Street*; Dr. Benjamin Graham (deceased) of *The Intelligent Investor*; Justin Mamis of *The Nature Of Risk*; Gordon Williamson of *Getting Started In Annuities*; Ben Baldwin of The *New Life Insurance Investment Advisor*; Professor Ruckstukl of the American College in Bryon Mawr, for his chapter titled: Investments and Investment Planning in *Fundamentals Of Financial Planning*, published by The American College; Dr. Alan Shapiro of *Modern Corporate Finance*; and W. Stansbury Carnes and Stephen Slifer of *The Atlas Of Economic Indicators*.

Many thanks also to Kristen Malone of KEH Data Services in Canyon Lake, California who typed and re-typed the chapters of this book. Any mistakes belong to the author.

CONTENTS

ABOUT THE AUTHOR

Eamonn "Ed" Nohilly's youth and schooling were spent far away, both geographically and mentally, from Wall Street and London, Great Britain's financial center. He was born in Galway, Ireland in 1949.

While his initial education in theology and a first career as a Franciscan Brother may not be the usual background for a financial consultant and author, it has in some unexpected ways shaped his approach to investment counseling.

In his 30s, several years after he had left the monastic order, Nohilly started his own casualty insurance agency, which he later expanded by including financial planning. This required him to study to obtain his securities license.

When Nohilly set out to enter the world of investing, he found no well-written books for the beginning investor. Thus he had to dig his way through dense, overly complex material. His struggle to understand investing has instilled him with an almost missionary commitment to helping the perplexed novice.

Nohilly has been an insurance agent for the past 25 years. He obtained his securities license in his early 40s. Shortly after obtaining his securities license, Nohilly decided that in his second career, he wanted to be an investment and personal finance author and educator for adult beginners. *Quarterback Your Investment Plan: The Basics For Beginners* is his first published book. The author hopes to have *Quarterback Your Financial Plan: The Basics For Beginners* published in the not too distant future.

This author believes that those who present investment and financial planning seminars usually overwhelm the attendees with more information than they are capable of making sense of. He also finds this true of most books available on these subjects. With his book *Quarterback Your Investment Plan*, Nohilly plans to help the novice investor overcome his or her mental fog with respect to understanding the basics about investing and the fundamentals of the major investment players (stocks, bonds, money market securities, savings accounts, mutual funds and residential real estate). He looks forward to further spreading such knowledge in an entertaining and provocative way through his book promotion efforts.

PART I

Your Coach's Game Plan

◆

Gaining Satisfactory Investment Yardage Is Much Easier Than Most People Think

CHAPTER
◆ 1 ◆

YOUR COACH'S GAME PLAN

Chances are that when you acquired important skills in your life, a coach, a teacher or a parent was there showing you form and technique, explaining the basics and guiding you through life's lessons. When you learned how to swim or play a sport, a coach of some sort showed you techniques for endurance or strategies for reaching a goal. Most of us have had teachers that have inspired us, helped us until a mental light went on, and we were suddenly able to understand a concept or a problem which had previously been in the dark for us. From our parents, most of us learned how to get along with others, to share, to tell right from wrong, to save money and many other important life skills.

Even with all the mentors you may have had in your life, it is quite likely that your education was entirely neglected in one important area—investing. You probably have had no one teach you the basics of this crucial skill—until now. In this book, I will serve as your investment coach, perhaps your first, as you begin to learn the key plays of the investment game.

What do a great coach, a great teacher and a great parent have in common? Each of them strives to accomplish three goals:

- To inspire the athlete, the student and the child to be the best possible, each according to his or her abilities.
- To give the athlete, the student and the child the basic information necessary to meet challenges and to present this information in a manner that the athlete, the student and the child clearly understands.
- To offer the athlete, the student and the child the right amount and quality of advice.

MY GOALS AS YOUR INVESTMENT COACH

As your investment coach, those are the three goals I've set out to accomplish over the next several chapters as you begin to learn the fundamentals of investing.

THE FIRST GOAL

First, I want to inspire you to believe in yourself, in your potential investment capabilities and in your ability to become a great quarterback of your investment plan. If today you are between the ages of twenty and sixty and consider yourself to be an absolute beginning investor, you may believe that the world of investing is far too complex for you to understand. That belief is likely to have stemmed from your school system's failure to offer even one course in investing during all your years of schooling. This misconception has also been thoroughly reinforced, time and time again, by the sea of unnecessarily complex financial information coming at you from television, newspapers, magazines, books, insurance and securities companies, investment seminars, mutual funds, as well as bank companies, and other financial institutions. You may have a mental block when it comes to understanding even the most basic concepts about investing and the major investment players.

Throughout this book, I will encourage you to be patient with yourself as you strive to overcome any mental block you may have about investing. As you go through the following chapters, you will probably find that your confidence in your investment ability will have risen dramatically in a very short period of time.

You can make great strides in understanding investment basics in a year or less—providing you begin today to follow these important steps:

- Learn the basics about investing and the major investment players—stocks, bonds, money market securities, savings accounts, mutual funds and residential real estate.
- Become familiar with the terminology that appears at the end of many chapters in this book.
- Implement at least some of the strategies explained near the end of each chapter.

THE SECOND GOAL

Second, as your coach, I will strive to present this information in a way that you can clearly understand. I am keenly aware of the challenges you may confront when you encounter the most basic investment concepts and investment players covered in this book. Unlike most financial writers, I did not demand that my mother get me the latest edition of the *Wall Street Journal* five minutes after my birth. I am aware of what it is like to feel overwhelmed because I lacked the knowledge needed to make wise financial decisions. This is simply not the case with the majority of financial writers and commentators.

Most investment and financial authors have known the basics about investing for as long as they can remember. This is a great obstacle to overcome when they attempt to explain investing in a way that adult beginners can clearly understand. The scarcity of excellent investment books for adult beginners demonstrates how many financial authors lack the insight to write from the novice investor's perspective. There are many excellent books written for those who know the basics about investing. Several of these books are recommended for your more in-depth reading towards the end of many chapters in this book.

THE NUMBER ONE REASON SO MANY FAIL FINANCIALLY

One financial author has asserted that there are six major reasons why so many fail financially. These six reasons have been cited by all kinds of people and financial institutions. The number one reason, according to her, is procrastination. Of the many absurd statements I have read and heard in my lifetime, this number one reason for why there are so many financial failures—procrastination—ranks up there at the top of the heap.

Until the day that all of us have the opportunity to learn the fundamentals about personal finance and investing through our schools and colleges, we should lay off the psychobabble and cancel the fishing expeditions for reasons why so many fail financially. Millions upon millions of people live in a sea of confusion about the investment players they may deal with throughout their adult lives. This state of affairs is perfectly understandable given that personal investing is not part of the curriculum in most U.S. schools.

THE NATION IS IN AN UPROAR

The nation is in an uproar because so many students graduate without knowing the basics in mathematics, writing and reading, but there is not a murmur about virtually all school graduates lacking knowledge about the basics of personal finance. Most politicians, including the President, claim that all high school graduates, from the year 2000, should be computer literate, but not a word has been uttered about teaching all—students and adults alike—to become financially literate.

We have many politicians and consumer protection crusaders pushing for laws, regulations and penalties to protect people from financial predators. However, we would be far better served if just one-tenth of that time were spent persuading schools to include one or more courses about personal finance in their curriculums.

THE THIRD GOAL

For my third coaching objective, I will strive to give you the right amount and quality of advice. That challenge is much more difficult than it looks. Most financial writers overwhelm the reader with the sheer quantity of their advice. Such authors drown readers in information beyond the capacity of novice investors to absorb and implement. The temptation to impart all one's knowledge, when the reader or listener is unprepared to comprehend most of it, is too great for most authors and commentators. For the majority of investment writers, it is probably accurate to say that there was not a time in their adult lives when they did not know the basics about investing. This was not true in my case. I did not know anything about the fundamentals of investing, or about the major investment players, until my early forties. Therefore, I will be very vigilant in giving you the right amount and quality of advice.

A PREVIEW OF CHAPTERS 2 THROUGH 17

Chapter 2, "Investing—A Useful Definition," shows the novice investor how difficult it is to understand the current world of investing because of the lack of clarity in the financial services industry about the words: betting, gambling, saving, speculating, trading and investing. The walls of separation, such as they are, are confusing and indeed counterproductive. A useful definition of investing will be presented. The challenge is then for you to execute an intelligent investment game plan, in light of this more pragmatic meaning and practical definition of investing.

Chapter 3, "Investment Risk—A New and Revolutionary Concept," introduces you to an essential and fundamental concept for every investor to clearly understand—risk. We will examine the generally accepted view of investment risk and the pyramid chart (see figure 1) typically used to illustrate the ascending scale of investment risk, which corresponds to this widely held idea of risk. In this chapter, we ask if this almost universally held view of investment risk is sound or fundamentally flawed. We discuss how acting under assumptions fostered by flawed definitions of risk can tragically mislead investors. Millions of people have made terribly unwise investment decisions because of a mistaken idea of risk.

The time has come for a practical and revolutionary concept of investment risk, one defined in relation to an individual investor's particular needs and circumstances. Chapter 3 will show you how to assess your risk and arrive at a meaning that is relevant for you. With this new understanding of risk, you should be able to make intelligent investment choices more easily in light of your personal and financial circumstances, the current and expected future market conditions and your future investment and financial goals.

Chapter 4, "An Overview of Your Major Investment Players," briefly describes how the major investment players can be divided into two basic approaches for gaining investment yardage—debt and equity investing—just as football can be divided into two basic ways of gaining offensive yardage—running and passing.

The three major debt investment players are:

- Bonds
- Money Market Securities
- Savings Accounts

The three major equity or ownership investment players are:

- Stocks
- Mutual Funds
- Residential Real Estate

Chapters 5 through 9 further introduce you to these investment players, which you should become familiar with now:

- Stocks
- Bonds
- Money Market Securities
- Savings Accounts
- Mutual Funds
- Residential Real Estate

Chapters 10 through 12 focus on tax advantaged investing and show how you can supercharge many investments through the wise use of our tax laws. These chapters discuss one of the most intelligent ways to invest can be through tax sheltered plans—such as a 401K, 403B, IRA, Roth IRA, Sep IRA, a Keogh Account, fixed and variable life insurance and fixed and variable annuities.

Chapter 10 explains the 401K, 403B, IRA and other tax sheltered plans.

Chapter 11 reviews fixed and variable life insurance.

Chapter 12 covers fixed and variable annuities.

Chapter 13, "Understanding the Economic News," is extremely important although it is not usually a separate chapter in beginning investment or financial planning books. It is not necessary to have a Harvard MBA to understand the basics of the economic news. Initially, just try to understand the major economic indicators and the role of the Federal Reserve Board. This chapter will help you to evaluate the current economic and expected future economic conditions that have such a powerful impact on the market value of various investments. Besides becoming a more intelligent investor, this little effort will help you become a more politically informed citizen and possibly less cynical than you may now be about our politicians and political parties.

Chapter 14, "Your Child's College Investment Plan," presents a surprising and easy-to-use strategy to help build your child's college investment plan. It shows how you can educate your child about investing through the Stock Market Game. By helping your child understand investing, you will have two heads, instead of one, working together on implementing an intelligent investment plan for his or her college education.

Chapter 15, "Investment Advisors—Who Should You Consult?," outlines the strategy you should follow in using investment advisors in your pursuit of becoming a great quarterback of your investment plan. The first group of investment and financial advisors you should hire—and the ones available for little money—can be found in the books I have recommended. Once you have read my book, have become familiar with most of the terminology and also read several books by specialty investment coaches, you will easily be able to decide what other investment advisors, if indeed any, you should consult in your quest to be a super quarterback of your investment plan.

Chapter 16, "The Eighth Wonder of the World Re-Examined," is a brief review of compound interest, which is often called "the eighth wonder of the world." But here we ask, "Is it indeed the eighth wonder of the world?" One day, especially if you are now in your twenties or thirties, you may proclaim compound interest "the eighth wonder of the world."

Chapter 17, "Your Investment Game Plan," lays out some basic strategies to encourage you to start today down the road to becoming a star quarterback of your investment plan. As we have just seen, the critical first step is to learn the fundamentals about investing and also about the investment players reviewed in this book. Everything else, including setting and writing down your investment objectives, is secondary. Young quarterbacks do not write down their goals on their first attempt at throwing the football. They first throw the football thousands of times and learn the fundamentals of the game. Very likely they watch and read about many football players who have become star quarterbacks. Only then do the dreams and goals start to take shape in their minds.

You should pursue a similar strategy. First, learn the fundamentals of investing and also the basics about the major investment players. Then, read several books written by specialty investment coaches such as: *One Up On Wall Street* by Peter Lynch with John Rothchild; *The Bond Book* by Annette Thau; and *Bogle on Mutual Funds* by John Bogle. *The New Money Masters* by John Train is a great source of information on how such investors as Peter Lynch, Philip Carret and John Neff became renowned in their field. These stories will inspire you to believe that you too can one day become a super quarterback of your investment plan.

May your riches multiply like the shamrocks in the bog and good fortune be your constant companion. (An old Irish proverb)

Your Investment Coach,
Eamonn "Ed" Nohilly

PART II

Investing Basics

CHAPTER

◆ 2 ◆

INVESTING

A Useful Definition

WHAT IS INVESTING?

Is opening a bank savings account investing? Is purchasing stocks or shares of a company investing? How about buying bonds—is it investing? Is buying money market securities investing? Is betting money on the horses investing? Is purchasing a state lottery ticket investing? Is playing bingo investing? Is purchasing a fixed universal life or a fixed deferred annuity investing? Is betting money on who will win the Super Bowl investing? Are any of these activities investing?

THE CURRENT PROBLEM

There are today no accepted, clear lines of demarcation that separate *investing, saving, gambling, betting, trading and speculating*. Whatever walls that may exist are confusing and counterproductive.

The time has come to echo the words (with just a slight variation) of President Reagan to Soviet Premier Mikhail Gorbachev at the Brandenberg Gate, overlooking the Berlin Wall, in 1985—"Tear down these walls."

We need to tear down these walls that now exist in the minds of most people regarding the words: *betting, gambling, saving, trading, speculating and investing*. We need a practical definition of investing that can help beginners to more easily understand the investment world.

MY DEFINITION OF INVESTING

Regardless of whether one is betting money on the horses, buying state lottery tickets, playing bingo, opening a savings account, buying undeveloped land, buying a fixed or variable annuity, purchasing stocks, bonds or mutual funds—all of these financial transactions have one important characteristic in common. They are all entered into with the expectation of obtaining a greater future financial return than the principal that was initially invested. Therefore, a useful definition of investing can be stated as follows: *It is an expenditure of money with the expectation of obtaining a greater return in the future.* That future could be in one second, one minute, one hour, one day, one year or fifty years. The time limit is determined by the investor.

AM I INVESTING INTELLIGENTLY?

The critical question is: Am I investing intelligently? In more precise terms, the question is: in light of my personal and financial circumstances, my investment and financial goals and the current and expected future market conditions, is there *compelling evidence* that I am making an *intelligent investment?* (The words "compelling evidence" are borrowed from what will surely become an investment classic *Bogle on Mutual Funds* by John Bogle and "intelligent investment" is from the recognized investment classic *The Intelligent Investor* by Dr. Benjamin Graham.)

How do you start meeting the challenge of deciding whether there is "compelling evidence" that you are making an intelligent investment? What are the major factors and variables that you should know and review in order to determine if your decision is wise?

WHERE DO YOU BEGIN?

First—You must have a basic knowledge of the most frequently used investment players. As a beginner, you should know the fundamentals about stocks, bonds, money market securities, savings accounts, mutual funds and residential real estate. Knowing the basics about these investment players should encompass the following:

14

● Knowing what each investment player is.

● Knowing the historic rates of investment returns of these players over the short and long-term. Consider short term as one year and long-term as greater than ten years.

● Knowing the chief reasons why the market value of these investment players fluctuate up or down over the short and long-term.

Second—You must know what your investment goal or goals are. Evaluate if these goals are reasonable in light of your circumstances, the current market and expected future market conditions. The rage in the business, academic and self-help world is to write down these goals. Although this strategy sounds laudable, it can be counterproductive. Too many people are advised to write down their investment and financial goals before they have a clue about what a stock, a bond or mutual fund is. Give yourself time in setting realistic investment and financial goals.

Third—You should realistically assess your personal and financial circumstances. Just as a football coach must constantly assess many variables in order to decide an intelligent game plan, you likewise must assess many variables in selecting an intelligent investment plan.

You need to take into account your age, marital status, occupation, current financial resources, investment time horizon, investment knowledge, tolerance and patience—or lack thereof—for the markets fluctuations and occasional volatility. Personal discipline and analytical ability are equally important factors to evaluate in order to determine if you are making an intelligent investment.

Fourth—You should have a good understanding of what the currently accepted theory of investment risk is and also my new and revolutionary concept. Both the usually accepted meaning of investment risk and my new and revolutionary definition are discussed in the next chapter titled "Investment Risk—A New and Revolutionary Concept."

Fifth—It is very important that you become familiar with and understand most of the investment terminology in this and the sev-

eral chapters that follow. Every discipline has its own terminology. Just look at the vast amount of terminology that has arisen from the computer field in such a short period of time. A unique feature of this book is the terminology section at the end of almost every chapter.

Sixth—You should have a basic understanding of the economic news in order to intelligently assess current market and expected future market conditions. This challenge is not as overwhelming as it may initially appear. Mastering or just becoming familiar with the major economic indicators and the role of the Federal Reserve Board will likely bring an end to what may now seem all too complex a subject for you to make any sense of.

Welcome to the world of investing and to the many challenges and opportunities it offers. As you navigate the sometimes turbulent waters of the investment world, be forever reassured by the words of Dr. Benjamin Graham:

> *To achieve satisfactory investment returns is much easier than most people realize.*

YOUR INVESTING GAME PLAN

Read and review the basics about the investment players discussed in the upcoming chapters, especially stocks, bonds, money market securities and mutual funds. Become familiar with most of the terminology at the end of this chapter and the other chapters in this book. By becoming familiar with these terms, you will soon be able to "decipher" what may now seem like a "secret code."

If you are new to the investing world, begin your investment portfolio through mutual funds. It is a superb way for rookies to start. Open-end mutual funds offer a magnificent opportunity to enter the investing world with confidence and with little money. Some mutual funds will accept as little as $1,000 to start and even much less if invested inside a qualified tax sheltered plan, such as a 401K, 403B, IRA and Roth IRA. Mutual funds are reviewed in Chapter 8.

Regardless of how small an investment portfolio you may have or how little money you may have to invest, always think of yourself as an investor. Never think of yourself as a saver, gambler, trader, bettor or speculator. If you are making an expenditure of money with the expectation of obtaining a greater financial return in the future, then you are an investor by my definition. By using this strategy, you will eliminate an enormous amount of confusion. You then only need to assess if you are making an intelligent investment.

For a better understanding of the investment world, read the following books:

➤ *Understanding Wall Street* by Jeffrey Little and Lucien Rhodes.

➤ *Guide to Investing* by Michael Steinberg.

➤ *Guide To Financial Independence* by Charles Schwab.

➤ *The Intelligent Investor* by Dr. Benjamin Graham.

Information about mail ordering these titles appears at end of this book.

INVESTING—TERMINOLOGY

Active Market - A high volume of trading in stocks and bonds or other securities. This high volume of trading may be in a particular stock, bond or other security.

Activity Charges - Charges that occur in many kinds of financial transactions. These charges are used to compensate a company. Every investor should investigate and know why there are any Activity Charges in their accounts.

After Tax Rate of Return - This is the net profit an investor receives after taxes are excluded from any investment gains.

American Depository Receipts (ADRs) - American Depository Receipts represent ownership rights in shares of foreign companies. They are traded every business day in the Over-The-Counter (OTC) market. U.S. investors do not directly buy shares in foreign corporations. Instead they buy them in the form of what's known as American Depository Receipts (ADRs). These ADRs are subject to currency fluctuations.

Annual Reports - Public corporations issue Annual Reports. In these reports is information that is of great value to many investors and mutual fund managers, among others. Beginning investors should only be aware of these reports. Later, if you wish, you can study them more in-depth.

Annual Return - This is the total return from an investment on an annual basis. It does not include any sales or other charges assessed. It does not reflect the rate of inflation or any taxes levied on investment earnings.

Asset Allocation - This is an investment expression that you will hear often. It simply means the amount of invested monies (assets) apportioned to each specific type of investment—such as stocks, bonds and money market securities. The amount of monies or assets that you should allocate to each type of investment player depends on many variables—including your age, occupation, financial resources, investment goals, tolerance or lack of tolerance for market fluctuations and even occasional volatility, knowledge of investing and of the major investment players and also your investment time horizon.

Balance Sheet - A statement issued by a corporation listing all its assets, liabilities and stockholders equity. It is of particular value to mutual fund managers. Beginning investors should be aware of what it is, but certainly need not become familiar with its details now.

Bears - This applies to investors who have a pessimistic outlook on the securities markets. Bears believe that stock prices will decline.

Bear Market - A stock market that shows larger than usual declining prices. One or two factors or even a multiplicity of factors could be the cause of a Bear Market.

Boiler Room - An expression used to describe any high pressure sales tactics employed to sell various products and services. Boiler Room sales people use "sucker lists" to prey upon the uninformed and vulnerable. A sure way of not being taken by Boiler Room sales tactics is to know at least the basics about investing and the major investment players.

Brokerage Firms - Companies that bring buyers and sellers together in the securities markets. Some well known brokerage firms are Merrill Lynch, Salomon Smith Barney, Charles Schwab, A.G. Edwards and Paine Weber. On occasion you may hear them referred to as "Broker/Dealers."

Bulls - This investment expression describes individuals who expect the stock market to increase in market value in the near future.

Capital Gains and Losses - The amount an investor has gained or lost from the sale of securities, such as stocks, bonds, or money market securities. It is the amount that the sales price differs from the cost price, excluding any expenses. Capital

Gains and Losses must be reported on Schedule D of Federal Income Tax Form 1040.

Capital Markets - These are the markets for long-term—greater than one year—debt and equity securities. You will hear and read about this term often. It usually will not be explained. The money market and capital market make up the financial market. It sounds more complex than it really is. That is why a familiarity with this terminology is so important.

Cash Equivalents or Cash Reserves - Assets that can easily be converted into cash without any loss of principal. Investment writers and reporters often interchange these terms. Sometimes they use the term "money market" without explanation in place of Cash Equivalents or Cash Reserves. Cash Equivalents, Cash Reserves and the money market offer a high degree of principal security at anytime and are also very liquid.

Cash Management Account - An account which brokerage firms, such as Merrill Lynch and Salomon Smith Barney, offer in combination with a checking account, money market account, credit and debit card and also a stock and bond account.

Debt Securities - Securities, such as bonds and money market investments, that represent a debt which must legally be repaid. Governments and corporations issue Debt Securities. Debt Securities are tradeable.

Discount Brokerage - A brokerage company, such as Charles Schwab and Quick and Reilly, that sells securities at a discount, compared to the full commission brokerage companies. More recently, "deep" Discount Brokerage companies have entered the financial scene.

Diversification - An investment strategy that avoids placing all your investment dollars in one "basket" or investment product. Moreover, investors who diversify their portfolios do not put all their invested dollars in one type of stock, such as technology or health. Diversifying your investment portfolio can be a very intelligent investment strategy. How a person should diversify his or her investment portfolio depends on many factors, such as the investor's age, financial resources, investment discipline, investment time horizon and investment knowledge.

Dividend - A part of a company's profit that is distributed to its shareholders by a vote of the board of directors. This is an investment term that you should become familiar with now—not later.

Dividend Reinvestment Plan - A plan that allows stockholders and mutual fund shareholders to reinvest automatically any dividends in additional shares or fractions of shares, usually at no cost or commission.

Equity Securities - Equity Securities represent an ownership right in a corporation. An example of an Equity Security is stocks. Equity Securities are tradeable.

Financial Market - The Financial Market is comprised of the money market and the capital market.

Investing - An expenditure of money with the expectation of obtaining a greater return in the future. This is how I define investing. You are welcome to disagree with it and make up your own definition! Rarely will financial or investment writers and commentators explain investing. This critical oversight unnecessarily confuses many beginning investors.

Liquidity - The ability to easily convert an investment into cash without any loss of principal.

Market Indexes or Averages - These are indexes that tell us how all or parts of the securities markets are doing every day. The most well known Market Indexes are associated with the stock market. Just about everybody has heard of the Dow Jones Industrial Average—commonly called the Dow. Other major Market Indexes or barometers of the stock market are the Standard and Poor's 500, Russell 2000 and Wilshire 5000. The Lehman Brothers Aggregate Bond Index is similar to the Wilshire 5000. It is a barometer or index of the whole bond market. The Wilshire 5000 is an Index or barometer of the whole stock market. The practice of *index investing* has become a very popular investment strategy in the past two decades. Make sure you learn more about this investment plan now. It makes investing intelligently so much easier, especially for beginning investors.

Market Volatility - A stock or bond market characterized by sharp swings in prices. A single factor or multiple factors can cause this Market Volatility. Stocks generally experience more Market Volatility than bonds. Money market securities fluctuate very little in market value because their maturity time is so short—one year or less.

Marketability - A security has Marketability if there is an active secondary market for it. For example, money market securities are very *marketable* because there are hundreds of thousands of buyers and sellers ready to trade money market securities every business day.

Moody's Investment Service - Moody's, just like Standard and Poor's and Fitch Investor Services, rates the creditworthiness of corporations and governments (both federal and state). These financial credit rating companies provide valuable information to investors, mutual fund managers and other individuals involved in making intelligent investment decisions.

NASDAQ – Refers to the computerized system of trading thousands of Over-The-Counter (OTC) stocks. The three major places that stocks are purchased and sold are the New York Stock Exchange (NYSE), the American Stock Exchange (AMEX) and NASDAQ. Both the NYSE and the AMEX are located in lower Manhattan in New York City. NASDAQ is not located in any one specific location. Rather, it is a computerized system of trading stocks.

Opportunity Cost - The investment opportunity one foregoes by selecting a specific course of action. A first time home buyer usually gives up opportunities to invest elsewhere because of the significant outlay of money needed to either make the down payment or monthly payments or both.

Paper Profit or Loss - A Profit or Loss that has not actually been realized. It is only on Paper so to speak. For example, a person may have a Paper Profit on their home since he or she purchased it ten years ago, but since the owner has not sold the house and netted the Profit, it is only a Paper Profit. The same is also true if it has lost market value since being purchased. It is only a Paper Loss.

Parking - A term that means a person is placing his or her money in an investment that offers a high degree of principal security and liquidity but little opportunity for growth, such as U.S. Treasury bills. Usually, an investor employs Parking until he or she decides where else to invest.

Primary Market - When a corporation sells its stocks for the first time, it sells them in the Primary Market. These stocks are then sold and purchased—traded—in the secondary market. As a beginning investor, the secondary market should become your primary concern. Later you can investigate the Primary Market.

Prime Rate - The interest rate banks charge their most creditworthy corporate customers. The Prime Rate charged by banks is very much affected by Federal Reserve Board interest rate changes. If you follow what the Federal Reserve Board is doing with interest rates, you will quickly become knowledgeable about how these changes affect so many other areas of the financial marketplace. The Federal Reserve is the central bank of the country.

Principal - The amount of money a person invests.

Prospectus - A lengthy document that a person must receive before investing in securities. Most of the information in a Prospectus is "boiler plate." It is common to all Prospectuses and required to be included by the Securities and Exchange Commission. Once you know the fundamentals about investing and the major investment players reviewed in this book, you will likely be able to focus quickly on the most important information in a Prospectus. You should read a Prospectus through from cover to cover at least once.

Securities - In the investment world Securities represent an ownership position in a corporation through owning shares of that corporation. They also express a debt position in either a corporation or government through bonds and money market securities. Usually, most people associate investing with the securities markets only. This is unfortunate and misguided. Purchasing a certificate of deposit (CD) or a fixed life insurance policy should equally be considered investing.

Securities and Exchange Commission (SEC) - The SEC oversees the enforcement of the nation's securities laws and protects the integrity of the securities market. For example, it requires full disclosure of all necessary information in a prospectus so that an investor can make an informed decision. By requiring full disclosure and observance of securities laws, the U.S. securities market is the most open and most trusted investment marketplace in the world. Many people have dedicated much of their lives to making sure we have fair, honest and open securities markets. The chairman of the Securities and Exchange Commission is appointed by the President.

Third Market - Stocks, bonds and money market securities are sold initially in the primary market. These securities are then traded—purchased and sold—in the secondary market. The

Third Market is for institutional investors who trade huge blocks of securities at any one time. This Third Market provides these institutional investors, such as insurance companies, mutual funds and pension funds, with a liquid marketplace and lower transaction and commission costs than the other markets.

Ticker Tape - Prior to computers, securities transactions were recorded on a Ticker Tape. These were rolls of paper that ticked as they went along because of the instrument used to record the data on the rolls. Just as the words "broken record" mean little to most young people, so too is Ticker Tape a relic of the past.

Total Return - An investment term you will see and hear often. It is the sum of dividends, interest and capital gains earned on an investment. It does not take into account any commissions or other charges. Many investors focus only on the total return instead of the real return. The real return takes into account commissions, other charges, inflation and taxes.

Trader - A person who buys and sells securities in order to make profits on very short-term price changes. Traders are usually distinguished from investors, but this can be more confusing than enlightening, particularly for beginning investors. Traders are investors by my definition of investing. The question is: are they intelligently investing?

Wall Street - An actual street in lower Manhattan. It is now the symbol of the U.S. securities markets and the center of capitalism. The New York stock Exchange (NYSE) opened on Wall Street in 1792.

CHAPTER

◆ 3 ◆

INVESTMENT RISK

A New and Revolutionary Concept

If you read any newspaper, financial planning or investment book, any money magazine—including *Worth*, *Forbes* and *Money*—or listen to any television or radio program discussion about investing, you will invariably encounter the word "Risk." As often as you read or hear "Risk" used, you'll probably never hear it defined or explained. Take my word for it now, but make a note to verify it later, that you'll find the proverbial needle in a haystack quicker than you'll find any financial writer or commentator attempt to define or explain what investment risk is.

Why is this? I don't know. Investment Risk is both a critical and fundamental investment concept to understand. My guess, and it is just a guess, is that virtually all financial writers and commentators believe they know "intuitively" what Investment Risk is and presume and believe that everyone else does too. Why, therefore, spend any time defining or explaining what all of us already know "intuitively?"

DO WE INTUITIVELY UNDERSTAND INVESTMENT RISK?

According to Dr. Alan Shapiro—author of *Modern Corporate Finance* (an academic textbook used in many universities and financial learning centers throughout the world):

Our intuition tells us that stocks are riskier than are corporate bonds, which in turn are riskier than are default-free government bonds. A long-term government bond, in turn, whose price fluctuates with interest rate movements, should be riskier than a Treasury bill, whose short term maturity largely insulates it from price variations.

Probably half of the adult population couldn't explain what a default-free government bond or a U.S. Treasury bill is, yet Dr. Shapiro still claims that we know "intuitively"—without deduction, logic or reasoning—that stocks are riskier than default-free government bonds and U.S. Treasury bills.

WHAT IS INVESTMENT RISK?

According to Professor William J. Ruckstukl at the American College in Bryn Mawr, Pennsylvania, investment risk is:

The variability in the expected return to be obtained from an investment. The greater the actual or perceived potential variation in the return, the greater is the risk of the investment.

For example, stocks always vary more in market value than thirteen-week U.S. Treasury bills. Therefore, according to Professor Ruckstukl, stocks are always riskier to invest in than short-term Treasuries. In fact, you will often read and hear that thirteen-week U.S. Treasury bills are risk-free or virtually risk-free investments and that stocks are risky investments. When investment writers and commentators use the word "Risk," and they do so often, it is likely this concept of investment risk that they are using.

BOGLE ON RISK

In his bestseller, *Bogle on Mutual Funds,* John Bogle devotes a chapter to "The Risks of Investing." He states:

That reward and risk go hand in hand is a commonplace. And both the rewards and risks of investing in a diversified common stock portfolio are, as a broad generalization, higher than those of the other two asset classes.

The other two asset classes John Bogle is referring to are bonds and money market securities. He does not define investment risk. However, when Bogle tells us that "the most widely accepted measure of the risk in any financial asset class is the volatility of its total returns," we can infer his agreement with Professor Ruckstukl's idea of investment risk.

OTHER DEFINITIONS OF INVESTMENT RISK

After much inquiry, I did find some other authors who did attempt to define investment risk. In *Modern Corporate Finance*, Dr. Alan Shapiro contends that:

> *Risk is usually thought of as the dispersion of possible outcomes around the expected return.*

Sylvia Porter, a well-known financial author and commentator, declares in *Sylvia Porter's—Your Finances In The 1990s*:

> *Professionals define risk for investment purposes as the 'percentage standard deviation of annual return'; in other words, the amount that the actual return tends to vary from the overall return.*

The New York Institute of Finance (NYIF) in its *Guide to Investing*, maintains that:

> *What we mean by risk is the certainty of return. An investment with a low certainty of return is considered to be high risk; an investment with a high certainty or probability of return on investment is considered to be a low risk.*

Business Week Magazine, in their 1992 *Guide to Mutual Funds*, assert:

> *For our scoreboard we define risk as the potential for losing money. There are other ways to define it, but for you as an investor, it is the most significant way.*

INVESTMENT RISK PYRAMID

On these widely accepted definitions, leading authorities have built the Investment Risk Pyramid, a frequently referenced graph that visually represents degrees of Risk. (See Figure 1, page 35.) While each Investment Risk Pyramid that you will see may not exactly duplicate the others, the pattern will be similar. The investments that fluctuate the least in market value will be at the bottom of the pyramid. These include passbook savings accounts, certificates of deposit (CDs), money market accounts, money market mutual funds, U.S. Treasury bills, fixed universal life, fixed deferred annuities and commercial paper. Investment players or products that historically have fluctuated the most in value will appear in the top section of the pyramid. Typically, what you are likely to see in this top section are undeveloped land, options, commodities, futures, gas and oil exploration.

Investment players that historically have fluctuated more or less in value than either of these two ends of the pyramid will appear in between.

Some pyramids will have three sections. Others may have four or five. The investment risk pyramid illustrated in Figure 1 has three sections.

IS THIS INVESTMENT RISK PYRAMID FUNDAMENTALLY SOUND?

Are these widely accepted definitions of investment risk and the graphically illustrated investment risk pyramid derived from them fundamentally sound? They have been accepted for so long by so many investors, financial learning centers, investment writers and commentators that it is almost impossible to imagine them as fundamentally flawed. It would be like Galileo challenging the theory that the earth is the center of the universe. Unthinkable. Let's, for a few moments, think the unthinkable and challenge the currently accepted concept of investment risk.

DR. GRAHAM ON THE CONCEPT OF RISK

This is what the greatest recognized investment educator—Dr. Benjamin Graham—in *The Intelligent Investor*— had to say on the Concept of Risk:

It is conventional to speak of good bonds as less risky than good preferred stocks and of the latter as less risky than common stocks. From this was derived the popular prejudice against common stocks because they are not "safe," which was demonstrated in the Federal Reserve Board's survey of 1948. We should like to point out that the words "risk" and "safety" are applied to securities in two different senses, with a resultant confusion in thought.

A bond is clearly proved unsafe when it defaults its interest or principal payments. Similarly, if a preferred stock or even a common stock is bought with the expectation that a given rate of dividend will be continued, then a reduction or passing of the dividend means that it has proved unsafe. It is also true that an investment contains a risk if there is a fair possibility that the holder may have to sell at a time when the price is well below cost.

(In the next several paragraphs Dr. Graham challenges the currently accepted concept of investment risk.)

Nevertheless, the idea of risk is often extended to apply to a possible decline in the price of a security, even though the decline may be of a cyclical and temporary nature and even though the holder is unlikely to be forced to sell at such times. These chances are present in all securities, other than United States savings bonds, and to a greater extent in the general run of common stocks than in senior issues as a class. But we believe that what is here involved, is not a true risk in the useful sense of the term....

we shall set forth our conviction that the bona fide investor does not lose money merely because the market price of his holdings declines; hence the fact that a decline may occur does not mean that he is running a true risk of loss. If a group of well-selected common-stock investments show a satisfactory overall return, as measured through a fair number of years, then this group investment has proved to be "safe." During that period, its market value is bound to fluctuate and as likely as not, it will sell for a while under the buyer's cost. If that makes the investment "risky," it would then have to be called both risky and safe at the same time. This confusion may be avoided if we apply the concept of risk solely to a loss of value which either is realized through actual sale, or is caused by a significant deterioration in the company's position—or, more frequently perhaps, is the result of the payment of an excessive price in relation to the intrinsic worth of the security.

Many common stocks do involve risks of such deterioration. But it is our thesis that a properly executed group investment in common stocks does not carry any substantial risk of this sort and that therefore it should not be termed "risky" merely because of the element of price fluctuation. But such risk is present if there is danger that the price may prove to have been clearly too high by intrinsic-value standards—even if any subsequent severe market decline may be recovered many years later.

RISK AND YOUR LUCKY LEPRECHAUN

Visualize for a moment the following hypothetical situation: it may help clarify Dr. Graham's concept of risk. Your lucky leprechaun is in front of you with two pots, not of gold, but of money. There is $10,000 in each pot, in exactly the same denominations. Both pots of money are the same in every respect. Here is the deal that the leprechaun offers you: you can keep either one of the pots, but only before you make a choice on an additional offer—you can toss a quarter one thousand times and every time the coin is heads, $50 will be added to the pot of money on your right and $10 will be added to the pot on your left. Every time it is tails, however, $10 will be taken away from the pot of money on your right but nothing will be taken away from the pot on your left. The choice is yours. Which offer are you going to select? Which of the two offers is riskier?

DR. GRAHAM'S CONCEPT OF RISK IN PRACTICE

If you select the pot on your right and the first toss of the quarter is tails, then $10 will be taken away from that pot. If you select the pot on your left and not only the first toss, but all 1000 tosses are tails, no money is taken out of that pot. In other words, by selecting the pot on your left, the principal—the $10,000—is guaranteed at all times. It is not guaranteed if you select the pot on your right.

According to the generally accepted concept of investment risk, it is riskier to select the pot on your right because you expose the principal—the $10,000—to a possible loss in value, regardless of how little that loss of principal may be or how short a time it may last. You do not expose the principal—the $10,000—to any loss by selecting the pot on your left.

Dr. Graham's concept of risk fundamentally disagrees with this commonly accepted concept of investment risk. Note once again the words of Dr. Graham, especially the last sentence:

. . .

the idea of risk is often extended to apply to a possible decline in the price of a security, even though the decline may be of a cyclical and temporary nature and even though the holder is unlikely to be forced to sell at such times.

. . .

we shall set forth our conviction that the bona fide investor does not lose money merely because the market price of his holdings decline; hence the fact that a decline may occur does not mean that he is running a true risk of loss. If a group of well-selected common-stock investments show a satisfactory overall return, as measured through a fair number of years, then this group investment has proven to be "safe." During that period, its market value is bound to fluctuate and as likely as not, it will sell for a while under the buyer's cost. If that makes the investment "risky," it would then have to be called both risky and safe at the same time.

. . .

it should not be termed "risky" merely because of the element of price fluctuation.

If you apply Dr. Graham's concept of investment risk to this leprechaun scenario, he would not conclude that selecting the pot on your right is riskier just because there may be a loss of part of the principal for a period of time. The loss of some of the principal, if indeed any at all, is only likely to last for a short period of time because with every toss of the coin that is heads, $50 is added to the pot on your right and only $10 is taken away from it, if the coin toss is tails. The laws of mathematical probability says that 1000 flips of a coin are likely to be 50% heads and 50% tails. It also says that the sequence of heads and tails will be in random order. The greater the number of coin tosses, the more likely it is over time that the pot on your right will increase more rapidly than by selecting the pot on your left.

Even though Dr. Graham's idea of investment risk is not in agreement with the generally accepted concept of investment risk, he does not offer us his definition in *The Intelligent Investor*. This, I believe, was a serious oversight on his part. As I have already stated, investment risk is both an important and fundamental concept for every investor to clearly understand.

INVESTMENT RISK PYRAMID

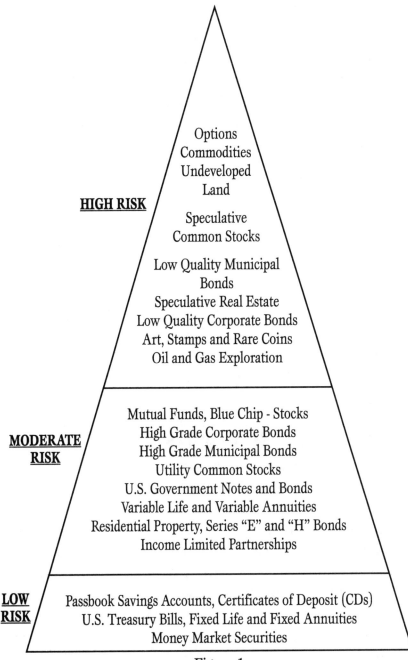

HIGH RISK

Options
Commodities
Undeveloped
Land

Speculative
Common Stocks

Low Quality Municipal
Bonds
Speculative Real Estate
Low Quality Corporate Bonds
Art, Stamps and Rare Coins
Oil and Gas Exploration

MODERATE RISK

Mutual Funds, Blue Chip - Stocks
High Grade Corporate Bonds
High Grade Municipal Bonds
Utility Common Stocks
U.S. Government Notes and Bonds
Variable Life and Variable Annuities
Residential Property, Series "E" and "H" Bonds
Income Limited Partnerships

LOW RISK

Passbook Savings Accounts, Certificates of Deposit (CDs)
U.S. Treasury Bills, Fixed Life and Fixed Annuities
Money Market Securities

Figure 1

IS THROWING THE BOMB RISKIER THAN A RUNNING PLAY?

If a person accepts Professor Ruckstukl's definition of investment risk as:

> *The variability in the expected return to be obtained from an investment. The greater the actual or perceived potential variation in the return, the greater is the risk of the investment.*

. . .

then that same person, if he or she has some familiarity with the game of football, would logically claim that throwing the bomb is riskier than a running play. After all, there is statistically a much greater variation in the returns from throwing the bomb than from running plays. What do you think? Is throwing the bomb riskier than a running play?

If I can demonstrate, just once, that throwing the bomb is *not* riskier than a running play, then I also prove that the generally accepted concept of investment risk is indeed fundamentally flawed? First I will prove that it is inaccurate to say that throwing the bomb—the long-yardage pass—is "riskier" than a running play. I will clearly show that a running play can be "riskier" than throwing the bomb.

IMAGINARY SUPER BOWL SCENARIO

Imagine the following Super Bowl scenario: the San Francisco 49ers are playing the Cincinnati Bengals. There are just two seconds left on the game clock. The 49ers have called their final time out to stop the clock. They are behind by four points. They have possession of the ball on the Bengals' forty yard line. There is time left for only one more play. The 49ers must score a touchdown in order to win. A field goal would leave them one point down. The Bengals' front line defense has been awesome. The 49ers have run into a virtual wall every time they have attempted a running play, but they are still in the game with a chance of winning. Unless the Bengals foul or the 49ers score a touchdown, the Bengals will win the Super Bowl on the next play. In this specific instance, which is a riskier play for the 49ers to exercise—throwing the bomb or a running play?

Can you imagine the 49ers scoring a touchdown with a running play in this situation? Their chances are virtually zero. The only possible chance the 49ers have of scoring a touchdown on this last play of the game, unless the Bengals foul, is with some passing play or the bomb.

Isn't it therefore logical to conclude, in this instance, that exercising a running play is riskier than throwing the bomb? Putting this in Maddenesque language (John Madden, the Fox Network sportscaster), it would be dumb to exercise a running play and very smart to throw the bomb!

HOW DOES A COACH DECIDE?

What is the factor or factors a coach would use, in this example, to determine if a running play is riskier than throwing the bomb or vice versa? The major determining factor is the goal to be achieved. In this case, it is crystal clear—the 49ers must score a touchdown. The second factor is the yardage gain needed to score a touchdown—forty in this situation. There are also other factors he would assess to determine the play option to exercise—such as field conditions, kind of players on each team and the variability in the returns from each kind of play.

Note that the variability in the returns from the various types of plays—running, passing and the bomb—is but one factor among several factors that a coach assesses in calculating the risk of the play to execute.

It is therefore incorrect to claim that throwing the bomb is riskier than a running play. What can be said with accuracy, with respect to the game of football, is that throwing the bomb is usually riskier than a running play, but not always. So—which is riskier—throwing the bomb or a running play? The answer—it depends.

PROFESSOR RUCKSTUCKL'S DEFINITION ONCE AGAIN

Let's return to Professor Ruckstukl's definition of investment risk. He asserts that investment risk is:

The variability in the expected return to be obtained from an investment. The greater the actual or perceived potential variation in the return, the greater is the risk of the investment.

Not only is it true from this definition of investment risk that stocks as a class are riskier than money market securities as a class but in fact any stock—even a blue chip stock—is always a more risky investment than a thirteen-week U.S. Treasury bill. Every stock has historically varied more in market value than thirteen-week Treasury bills. In no instance, according to the generally accepted concept of investment risk, is it ever riskier to invest in thirteen-week Treasury bills than to invest in a no-load index mutual fund that replicates the Standard and Poor's 500 or Wilshire 5000.

GENERALLY ACCEPTED CONCEPT OF INVESTMENT RISK

What is the risk in investing? According to Business Week Magazine's 1992 *Guide to Mutual Funds*, it is "the potential for losing money."

The risk is the exposure of the invested principal to a loss in market value, regardless of how little that loss in principal may be, and also regardless of how short in duration that reduction in principal may last.

NOTHING ABOUT THE INVESTOR IS A FACTOR

Under the currently accepted theory of investment risk, the investor's goal is not a factor in the riskiness of an investment. In fact, if you analyze it closer, you will find that nothing about the investor is a factor in determining the risk of an investment. That's correct—nothing at all. Not the investor's age, knowledge of investing, tolerance or lack of tolerance for market fluctuations and occasional volatility, financial circumstances, investment time horizon, job stability, investment discipline, analytical ability, investor's knowledge of current market conditions and expected future market conditions. None of these are factors in calculating the risk of an investment. The only factor is:

. . .

the variability in the expected return from an investment. The greater the actual or perceived potential variation in the return, the greater is the risk of the investment.

CURRENT INVESTMENT RISK THEORY IN PRACTICE

Based on the common understanding of investment risk, it can be said that Warren Buffett (a name you should become familiar with), someone who has made a fortune investing in stocks, is taking exactly the same investment risk by buying $200,000 worth of GEICO stock (he currently owns most of this company's stock) as a couple in their 70s who also buy $200,000 worth of GEICO stock, which is every dime of their current financial resources. This couple have invested all their financial resources in GEICO stock, based on the advice of a trusted friend who knows little about investing, but convinces them that if the recognized greatest stock market investor is buying GEICO stock, it would be very wise for them to do the same.

Unlike Warren Buffett, this retired couple have almost no tolerance for stock market fluctuations, not to mention its occasional volatility. Yet, by the currently accepted concept of investment risk, they are taking exactly the same risk with their $200,000 worth of GEICO stock as Mr. Buffett is with his purchase of $200,000 worth of GEICO stock. Is this absurd or what? It is in fact worse—it is tragic.

IT IS FUNDAMENTALLY AND TRAGICALLY FLAWED

The current accepted concept of Investment Risk is not only fundamentally flawed, but because people are living many more years after retirement, it is potentially tragic. Millions of people have made terribly unwise investment choices because of a misleading understanding of risk. Millions will continue to do so until they are able to discover a more practical definition of investment risk.

Millions of people have invested their monies in certificates of deposit, short-term Treasuries and other money market investments, believing them to be virtually risk free. Because of their flawed understanding of investment risk, they have left themselves potentially exposed to the financial possibility of not having adequate financial resources to live the lifestyle they had hoped and expected during their golden years. Had they instead acted on a more practical understanding of investment risk and invested even 60 % to 70 % of those same monies in a no-load index mutual fund that replicates the Wilshire 5000 or Standard and Poor's 500, through dollar-cost-averaging, they would probably be able to live their retirement years as they had planned.

TIME AND THE COMPOUNDING OF INVESTMENT RETURNS

Two important factors would likely have caused this to happen. First, investing in common stocks, as a class, have historically yielded much greater financial returns over the long-term than either bonds or money market securities. Second, the compounding of those greater returns over an extended period of time, would have a profound positive effect on their investment portfolio both before and during their retirement years.

BEST EXAMPLE OF THIS FLAWED CONCEPT OF RISK

The greatest personification I have seen of how tragically flawed the present theory of investment risk is was graphically illustrated. (See Figure 2, Page 42.) in an investment book for beginners published in 1994 by Christy Heady titled: *The Complete Idiot's Guide to Making Money on Wall Street*. There are five tiers in this investment risk pyramid, which as I indicated earlier, is not of much significance. Quite often these pyramids are illustrated with three or four sections. The concept is still the same. Note the comment the author makes at the top of each section. It is my opinion that most people, who for most of the time have the majority of their investment dollars in the bottom tier, that they ought to be clearing out the local pharmacy of pepto bismol instead of getting a good nights rest. It is also my opinion that most people, who for most of the time have most of their investment dollars in the third and fourth tier from the bottom, that they ought to be having a very restful nights sleep with very little tossing and turning. And yes, the top section of investment players—options, gold, futures, commodities, sector funds and junk bonds—can play an intelligent role in some investors game plan, without interfering with their getting a great nights sleep. There are also many people who have all their invested dollars in the second tier— that is U.S. federal agency bond funds, U.S. government securities, money market mutual funds and savings bonds—who should be staying up all night trying to figure out how to more intelligently invest their money, in light of their personal and financial circumstances and also their future investment and financial goals.

WARREN BUFFET

In his preface to *The Intelligent Investor*, (Revised edition published in 1973) Warren Buffett states:

> *To invest successfully over a lifetime does not require a strato-spheric IQ, unusual business insights, or inside information. What's needed is a sound intellectual framework for making decisions and the ability to keep emotions from corroding that framework.*

We do not have "a sound intellectual framework for making decisions" as long as we adhere to the currently accepted concept of investment risk. We must find a practical and revolutionary understanding of investment risk, in order to provide a "sound intellectual framework for making decisions." To that end, the rest of this chapter is devoted.

INVESTMENT RISK PYRAMID

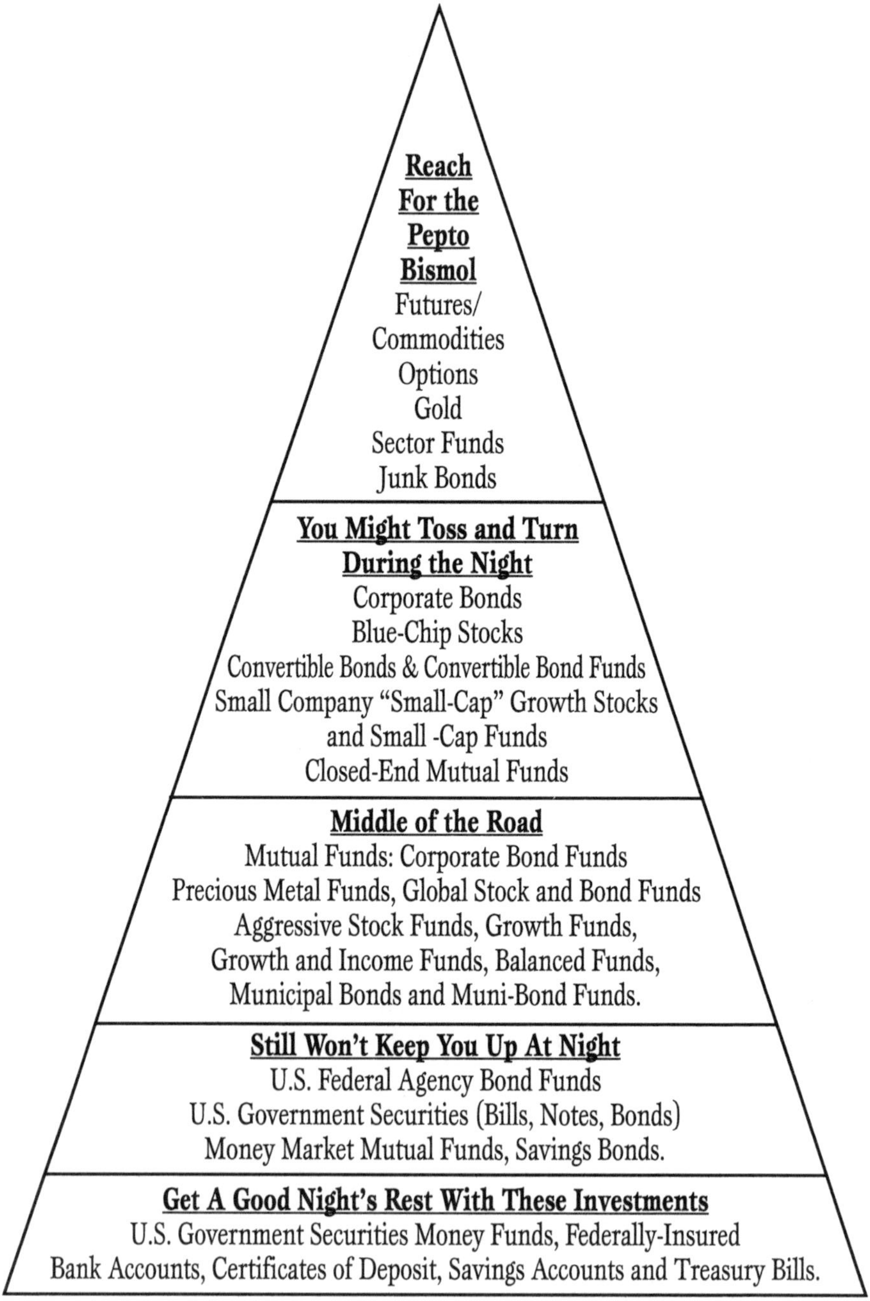

**Reach
For the
Pepto
Bismol**
Futures/
Commodities
Options
Gold
Sector Funds
Junk Bonds

**You Might Toss and Turn
During the Night**
Corporate Bonds
Blue-Chip Stocks
Convertible Bonds & Convertible Bond Funds
Small Company "Small-Cap" Growth Stocks
and Small -Cap Funds
Closed-End Mutual Funds

Middle of the Road
Mutual Funds: Corporate Bond Funds
Precious Metal Funds, Global Stock and Bond Funds
Aggressive Stock Funds, Growth Funds,
Growth and Income Funds, Balanced Funds,
Municipal Bonds and Muni-Bond Funds.

Still Won't Keep You Up At Night
U.S. Federal Agency Bond Funds
U.S. Government Securities (Bills, Notes, Bonds)
Money Market Mutual Funds, Savings Bonds.

Get A Good Night's Rest With These Investments
U.S. Government Securities Money Funds, Federally-Insured
Bank Accounts, Certificates of Deposit, Savings Accounts and Treasury Bills.

Figure 2

THE WORD RISK AS USED IN EVERYDAY LIFE

Let's first examine the word risk itself as used in everyday life. Most people, if asked, would likely say that risk means danger, hazard, peril, the probability of a loss or some adverse outcome. They would see nothing positive or potentially positive about risk. Justin Mamis, in his book titled *The Nature Of Risk* asks:

> *How does one use risk positively? Let's examine one daily life situation—crossing the street—to see what the risks are: When risk is examined in terms of the moment-to-moment decisions—stepping off the curb being an assumption of risk with all the dictionary negatives of hazard, peril, exposure to danger, but also with a positive: to get successfully to the other side—risk is at its core making a choice.*

Later he states that risk:

> . . .

> *is no more positive than it is negative. It isn't anything emotional at all. The dictionary is wrong: risk is a choice.*

NEW DEFINITION OF INVESTMENT RISK

If risk is a choice, as Justin Mamis claims, then what is investment risk? Isn't it making an investment choice? What is the outcome of making that investment choice? There are two possibilities—one is that an investor achieves his or her investment goal and the other is that he or she does not achieve his or her investment goal. Of course, an investor could have more than just one goal. Based on what has just been stated, *investment risk is a choice made that offers the possibility of achieving or not achieving your investment goal or goals.*

If investment risk is a choice that offers the possibility of achieving or not achieving your investment goal or goals, what then is the variability in the expected returns to be obtained from the various investment players? What does one call the variability in the expected returns from the two major offensive football plays—running and passing? There is no name that I'm aware of. The variability in the returns from the various offensive plays is simply a characteristic of the game. What one can say with accuracy about the game of football is that every coach assesses the variability in the expected returns from the various offensive plays as a factor, among many of other factors, in determining an intelligent offensive game plan. So should you in trying to determine an intelligent investment game plan. You should consider the variability in the returns of each investment player, over the short and long-term, as well as many other factors in determining an intelligent investment game plan.

DRAWING THE WRONG CONCLUSION

To say that investing in common stocks is always riskier than investing in U.S. Treasury bills or FDIC insured certificates of deposit is to attribute to stocks a characteristic that does not exist and is indeed tragically false. It is the same as saying that the sun or rain are dangerous. Yes, we know that exposure to the sun, without sun protection, over a long period of time, can cause cancer. Yes, we know that extremely heavy rains can cause flooding and as a result of that flooding, possible death and property destruction. But without the sun and rain there would be no human life.

Similarly in the investment world. Downside possibilities can occur only when we enter into the investment game. But only when we enter the investment world can we discover rewarding investment opportunities. What do we want to accomplish in playing the investment game? We can only assess the downside or danger and the upside or possibilities by first knowing what we realistically want to accomplish. It is worth repeating what has already been stated by the legendary investor—Warren Buffett:

> *What's needed (to invest successfully over a lifetime) is a sound intellectual framework for making decisions and the ability to keep emotions from corroding that framework.*

HOW TO REVIEW YOUR UPCOMING INVESTMENT PLAYERS

Read about the investment players discussed in the upcoming chapters. Do so without attributing or imputing any preconceived or emotional characteristics to them. Become familiar with their terminology. Acquaint yourself with the historical rates of return of these investment players over the short and long-term. Learn the basic characteristics of each and also why each investment player fluctuates more or less in market value over both the short and long haul. Become familiar with current market conditions and expected future market conditions. To do this, you must learn the about our economy. Try to intelligently assess your own personal and financial circumstances. The challenge ahead may seem daunting but always be aware that to gain satisfactory investment yardage is much easier than most people think.

YOUR INVESTMENT RISK GAME PLAN

Take your time to get a clear understanding of what virtually all financial writers and commentators mean when they use the words "risk" "risky" or "riskiness."

Note that in the terminology section that follows, the word risk is defined to mean the possibility of a financial loss, with the exception of Professor Ruckstukl's and Eamonn Nohilly's definition. There is nothing potentially positive in its usage.

INVESTMENT RISK—TERMINOLOGY

Certain words can be extremely important. Make sure you question and analyze what investment writers and commentators mean when they use particular words. I cannot emphasize this enough. Do not presume that just because they are "authorities" on investing that they have really thought through every word or phrase. They have not.

The word "risk" in all of the following glossary of investment terms, with the exception of two—Professor Ruckstukl's and my own—will be defined and used in the usual manner. It will be used to mean hazard, danger or the possibility of some kind of financial loss or adverse outcome. There will be nothing positive or potentially positive in its usage. After seeing how it is usually used and how I define investment risk, you will then be in a position to judge which definition would make most sense for you to ascribe to in your future investment plans. Of course you could come up with your own definition. Good luck!

Default Risk - The danger or downside possibility that a borrower, such as a corporation, will default or not pay its interest payments. It may even default or fail to pay the principal as well.

Downside Risk - The downside danger or possibility of financial loss because of a particular investment decision. For example, it is often said that investing in thirteen-week U.S. Treasury bills has no downside risk because you cannot "lose" your money. If this is only referring to a loss of principal, then certainly it is true to say that you cannot "lose" your investment principal by purchasing thirteen-week U.S. Treasury bills. If, on the other hand, you define "lose" to mean any loss in the purchasing power of your invested dollars, then you certainly can "lose" money by investing in thirteen-week Treasury bills.

Exchange Risk - The downside possibility or danger of suffering investment losses due to foreign currency exchange rates fluctuating.

Interest Rate Risk - The danger or downside possibility that interest rate changes by the Federal Reserve Board may adversely affect an investment portfolio. One investor's good news about Federal Reserve Board interest rate changes may be another's bad news. Usually it is good news for stock market investors when the FRB reduces short-term interest rates and bad news for many retirees who are heavily dependent on the interest earnings from their short-term debt investments, such as CDs or money market securities.

Investment Risk (Eamonn Nohilly's Definition) - It is a choice made that offers the possibility of achieving or not achieving your investment goal or goals.

Investment Risk (Professor Ruckstukl of the American College) - The variability in the expected return to be expected from an investment. The greater the actual or perceived potential variation in the return, the greater is the risk of the investment.

Liquidity Risk - The danger or downside possibility that an investor may not be able to sell his or her securities or other investments without selling at a loss. Money market securities have little Liquidity Risk. They can be sold easily without any loss in principal.

Market Risk - The danger or downside possibility that the market value of securities will decrease significantly and at the wrong time. Stocks, for example, are subject to greater Market Risk than money market securities.

Principal Risk - The danger or downside possibility that a person's invested money will decrease, regardless of how little a decrease in principal it may be or how short in duration that loss in principal may last. Too many investors focus only on this possibility. Of course, it can now be said, because of the growing popularity of day trading and other investment practices, that many investors are overlooking the fact that they could lose all of their invested principal.

Purchasing Power Risk - The danger or downside possibility that a person's investment portfolio will not appreciate in value enough to overcome the terrible twins—taxes and inflation. Far too few people focus on this possibility. Too many investors focus only on the possible loss of even just a part of their principal, even if that small loss in principal may last only for a short period of time.

Reinvestment Risk - The danger or downside possibility that a person may not be able to reinvest interest earnings, dividends and capital gains at a rate that he or she was achieving earlier. For example, a person who invests in a one-year certificate of deposit, instead of a three-year certificate of deposit, may find that interest rates have declined during the year. Therefore, he or she will be unable to earn the same interest rate for the following year or two, on renewing the CD.

Risk (As Generally Understood) - Danger, hazard, peril or the downside possibility or probability of some kind of loss or adverse outcome. Note that there is nothing potentially positive in the meaning usually conveyed by the word risk.

Risk Averse - An investor who is unwilling to expose his or her investment portfolio to market fluctuations and its occasional volatility. Many investment writers and commentators recommend that such a person invest in money market securities and bank savings accounts. They give this advice without warning the investor that he or she may very well be going into the "lions den." The purchasing power of a person's invested dollars is likely to decline with such a strategy. This could have disastrous consequences for millions of people, particularly during their retirement years.

Risk Measures - Theories that use complex mathematical computations to measure the variability in the expected returns to be obtained from specific investments. Some of these theories go by the names of "standard deviation," "coefficient of variant" and "beta." Just be familiar with these words. Do not read up on them now. Later maybe. If you do, be prepared to go into a "London Fog" that you may never come out of!

Risk Return - A central concept under currently accepted *investment risk* theory. It simply says that an investment that fluctuates more in value than another investment should provide a greater return. This concept of investment risk does not take into account any personal factor about the investor, such as the investor's age, occupation, financial resources, knowledge of investing, tolerance or lack of tolerance for market fluctuation and occasional volatility or investment time horizon.

Tax Risk - The danger or downside possibility that after taxes are levied on investment gains, the purchasing power of a person's investment portfolio will have significantly reduced. Every person should seriously investigate the tax consequences of their investment planning. Many investors give little consideration to this area.

Volatile Market - A securities market that is characterized by rapid and usually unforeseen fluctuations. Many investors worry unnecessarily about short-term market fluctuations and volatility even though they have intelligently decided to invest for the long-term. They should be getting a good nights rest during such times, rather than emptying out the local pharmacy of antacids.

PART III

Your Major Investment Players

◆

A Powerful Offense

CHAPTER
◆ 4 ◆

AN OVERVIEW OF YOUR MAJOR INVESTMENT PLAYERS

TWO WAYS OF GAINING FOOTBALL YARDAGE

We know that the game of football uses primarily two basic strategies to gain yardage—running and passing plays. Most of the "chicken scratchings" that Fox Network's John Madden and other football sportscasters sketch on your television screen when they discuss various offensive plays, diagram either running or passing plays. Running plays are exercised in order to gain consistent but not very long yardage. Occasionally, long yardage is gained with running plays. Sometimes yardage is lost. In today's game of football, a team that wants to gain significant yardage must go to the air. They must pass the football and occasionally throw the bomb. No modern team will win the Super Bowl without a major passing game.

TWO WAYS OF GAINING INVESTMENT YARDAGE

We can compare gaining investment yardage to the offensive game in football. There are two basic ways of achieving investment "yardage"—debt and equity investing. Think of debt investing as similar to the running game in football and equity investing as resembling the passing game.

DEBT INVESTING IS LENDING YOUR MONEY

Debt investing, at its basic level, is simply getting paid interest for lending money to someone or some entity, such as the U.S., state and local governments, corporations, banks and insurance companies. The money lent, commonly called the principal, is agreed to be returned at a specific time. This, as I just stated, is investing through debt at its most elementary level. It does, of course, get more involved than this. You should learn the basics about the following three debt investment players:

- Bonds
- Money Market Securities
- Savings Accounts

Bonds are the second investment player reviewed in the upcoming chapters. Money market securities and savings accounts are the third and fourth investment players examined. They are critiqued in the same chapter because they have many similar characteristics. It is not as difficult as you may now assume to learn the essentials about investing through debt. Learn the fundamentals about bonds, money market securities and savings accounts and you will be well on your way in determining what role debt investing should play in your investment plan. You may be surprised at the ease with which you can call your own investment plays. I've known the feeling of intimidation that so-called investment experts can evoke in beginning investors.

DEBT INVESTING IS SIMILAR TO THE RUNNING GAME

Think of debt investing as resembling the running game in football. The historic record of the past seventy-five years conclusively shows that a person should only expect to gain short to medium investment yardage through debt investing. Occasionally, you can gain long investment yardage through debt investing. Later, when you understand how Federal Reserve Board interest rate changes affects the market value of bonds, you will see how a person can sometimes achieve long investment yardage through debt investing.

EQUITY INVESTING IS BEING AN OWNER

The other major method of investing, besides debt investing, is equity investing. When you see or hear the words *equity investing* or *equities*, think of the word *ownership*. Investing in equities is investing in ownership players. The three equity or ownership investment players that you should learn the fundamentals about are:

- Stocks
- Mutual Funds
- Residential Real Estate

At the outset, learn the fundamentals about stocks. They are the first investment player reviewed in the upcoming chapters.

Understanding stocks, bonds and money market securities will prepare you to more easily comprehend mutual funds. Once you have grasped the fundamentals about stocks, bonds, money market securities, savings accounts and mutual funds, you will see how easily you can turbocharge those investment yardage gains through tax sheltered plans. Tax sheltered plans include: 401K, 403B, IRA, Roth IRA, Keogh plan, fixed and variable life insurance and fixed and variable annuities.

EQUITY INVESTING IS SIMILAR TO THE PASSING GAME

Think of investing in equities, or *ownership investment players*—these include stocks, mutual funds and residential real estate—as similar to the passing game in football. You can gain medium to long investment yardage by investing in equities. Investing in equities, over the long run, have yielded much greater investment yardage gains than investing through debt. This historic pattern of debt versus equity investment returns is likely to continue. Once you know the fundamentals about the investment players reviewed in this book, and have read just some of the books that I have recommended for your more in-depth reading, you will be in as good a position as anyone to determine if the historic investment yardage returns of the past seventy-five years are likely or not to continue in this century.

THE IMPORTANCE OF TIME

When approaching the basics about the major investment players that you should become familiar with now, keep in mind the one important difference between investing and football—the concept of time. In the game of football, time can be compacted into extremely short periods. It often is critical that a team accomplish a particular objective on the next play. Very often, because of the score, the clock becomes an enemy. Time is compressed, so to speak, in the game of football in order to make the game more exciting for players and fans alike.

In the game of investing, it is unrealistic to expect great investment yardage gains if you do not have a significant amount of time to invest— at least 15 years—regardless of your knowledge level. When retirement seems to be on the very distant horizon, and you do not have a clue what a stock, a bond, or a money market security is, it is difficult to understand the importance of this concept of time in gaining significant investment yardage. Once you know the ABCs about the investment players reviewed in this book and have seen their historic rates of returns over the past seventy-five years, you will easily understand the vital importance a long-term investment horizon can play in your becoming a great quarterback of your investment plan. For now, as a beginner it is important that you first focus your time on learning the fundamentals about the major investment players. Having done that, you then can center your time on learning the other basics. One fundamental—the concept of time—is key to making satisfactory investment yardage gains.

THE HISTORIC RATES OF INVESTMENT RETURNS

Take a look in Appendix 1 and you will see a graph that shows the historic rates of return of stocks, bonds and U.S. Treasury bills since 1925. It also shows the historic rate of inflation since 1925. This graph is provided by the esteemed Ibbotson Associates in Chicago. It is one of the most reputable and reliable investment data sources in this country.

CHAPTER
◆ 5 ◆

STOCKS

Great Yardage Gainers

For an NFL team to gain long yardage, they usually have to go to the air. That is, they must pass the football and occasionally throw the bomb.

HOW TO GAIN LONG INVESTMENT YARDAGE

If you want to gain long investment yardage, you should invest in common stocks. Achieving long yardage in the investment world means that the total returns on your invested dollars is much greater than the rate of inflation and taxes combined. The taxes we are referring to are those levied on capital gains, interest earnings and dividends. Overwhelming historical evidence shows that you cannot consistently gain long yardage in the investment game with "running plays." "Running plays" in the investment game include: passbook savings accounts, certificates of deposit, fixed life insurance, fixed annuities and money market securities. Ironically, these are the same investments that most authors place in the bottom tier—the lowest risk category—of the typical investment risk pyramid.

Millions of people have gone into their retirement years with a very small investment portfolio mainly because they had no idea how to overcome the terrible twins—taxes and inflation. The little investment yardage gained with money market securities, savings accounts and certificates of deposit is usually obliterated by taxes and inflation. In fact, many people have lost yardage because the purchasing power of their invested dollars declined. Investment yardage is lost mainly because people do not know the basics about stocks and stock mutual funds and because of the prevailing but flawed concept of investment risk. Beginning investors have commonly accepted this concept because it is preached as gospel by virtually all financial writers and commentators.

Let's now explore the great investment yard gainers—stocks. As we examine their characteristics, you will likely see what an important part they can play in helping you to be a super quarterback of your investment plan.

WHAT ARE STOCKS?

Stocks, or shares as they are often called, represent a proportional ownership of a corporation. The greater the number of stocks of a corporation a person owns, the greater is their ownership of that corporation. In fact, a person who owns more than 50% of the shares of a corporation has control of the company. He or she can fire the sitting board of directors and hire new ones. A person who owns stock in a corporation is said to have an equity or ownership position in that corporation. That is why you will often hear stocks referred to as equities.

You may be wondering how a person who owns just one share of say McDonald's, IBM, Microsoft or General Electric, out of millions upon millions of shares outstanding, could have ownership rights in these companies. But they do. Once you read *One Up On Wall Street* by Peter Lynch with John Rothchild, and some of the other books that are recommended later in this chapter, you will feel as if you had understood this concept all your life. The idea that stocks or shares represent a proportional ownership of a corporation will seem quite logical to you.

TWO TYPES OF CORPORATIONS

There are two types of corporations. One is a public corporation and the other is private. Most corporations are private. The stocks of private corporations are not traded publicly. When we refer to the stock market, we are only referring to the stocks of publicly traded corporations. Anyone can buy shares of these publicly traded corporations. Not so with private corporations.

INITIAL PUBLIC OFFERING

Corporations decide to go public, that is they sell their shares or stocks to the public, for basically one reason—to raise money for expansion in order to make greater profits. When a corporation offers its stock for sale to the public, it is said, in the language of the marketplace, to be "going public" or making an initial public offering—IPO for short. Rarely does an individual investor get an opportunity to buy stocks at an initial public offering (IPO), particularly if it is the shares of a corporation that is sought after by mutual funds, pension funds, insurance companies and other major financial institutions.

Some wealthy individuals, with connections, can do so from time to time. This is no investment handicap for the beginning investor, because under almost no circumstances should a beginning investor be purchasing stocks at an initial public offering (IPO). The knowledge of beginning investors is such that buying IPO offerings, even if they could purchase such shares, would not be wise. Those stocks that are sold at an IPO are sold in the primary market. Once stocks are sold in the primary market, they are then purchased and sold in the secondary market. The monies a corporation earns in an IPO after expenses are now utilized by the board of directors in the best manner they see fit for the company's expansion.

THE SECONDARY MARKET

The secondary market dwarfs the primary market. For the most part, it is the secondary market that is talked and written about every day in the broadcast media, financial press and various money magazines. You should now become familiar with the secondary market. Later, when you have some experience investing, you can investigate the primary market further.

In the secondary market, where stocks are traded—that is purchased and sold—after being initially sold in an IPO, hundreds of millions of stocks are traded every business day. The U.S. stock market is currently the largest and most competitive in the world. Virtually all stocks are traded through a stockbroker. There are some public corporations that you can now purchase stocks directly from without utilizing a stockbroker. For advanced reading on this method of stock market investing read *Buying Stocks Without A Broker* by Charles Carlson.

METHODS OF TRADING STOCKS

The two most well-known methods of trading stocks are through full service brokers and discount brokers. The major full service stock brokerages include Merrill Lynch, Morgan Stanley Dean Witter, Salomon Smith Barney, A.G. Edwards, Prudential Securities, Crowell-Weedon and Co., Paine Weber and Scudder-Kemper. The major discount stock brokerages are Charles Schwab, Quick and Reilly and Fidelity Investments. Discount brokers transact stock trades at a lower cost or commission than full service stock brokerage houses. Discount stock brokerage houses offer little financial advice. Full service brokerages will answer many questions that investors have. People who feel comfortable and confident about making their own investment decisions use the services of discount brokers instead of full service brokers.

Regardless of whether one uses a full service brokerage, such as Merrill Lynch and Prudential Securities or a discount brokerage, like Charles Schwab or Fidelity Investments, all brokerages have registered representatives answering the phones. A registered representative must pass a test, called *Series 7*, that is administered by the National Association of Securities Dealers (NASD), in order to obtain their securities license and buy and sell stocks on behalf of a stockbroker. You may occasionally hear a registered representative say he or she is a stockbroker by profession. Technically, this is not true. They are only the agents of the stockbroker—such as Merrill Lynch, Paine Weber or Charles Schwab.

THREE MAJOR STOCK EXCHANGES

There are three huge stock exchanges where most of these stocks trade. The most famous is the New York Stock Exchange—NYSE for short. The others are the American Stock Exchange—called the AMEX—and NASDAQ, which stands for National Association of Securities Dealers Automated Quotation System. NASDAQ is said to be the over-the-counter market. Originally, stocks on NASDAQ were traded over a counter, so that is how the term "over-the-counter" came into being. No actual building houses NASDAQ, unlike the New York Stock Exchange (NYSE) and the American Stock Exchange (AMEX), which are located in lower Manhattan in New York City. This area of New York City is called Wall Street. There is today an actual street called "Wall Street" in lower Manhattan, but when financial writers, commentators and investors refer to Wall Street, they mean the securities markets where stocks, bonds and other investments are traded.

WHAT DRIVES STOCK PRICES?

Take a look at any graph (see Appendix 1 at the end of this book) of stock market prices over a long period of time and you will see something obvious—their prices or values have gone up and up. You will also note that stock market prices have not increased at exactly the same rate every year, nor every ten or thirty years for that matter.

You can see that their price fluctuations can sometimes be quite volatile. What causes this to happen? Sometimes the answer is easy. Often, even for recognized stock market experts, the answer is elusive. It is similar to the game of football. To those who have a basic knowledge of the game and the teams, it seems apparent why one team has a good season and another a poor one. But even for experts of the game, it is often a mystery to them why a particular team lost or won a specific game, or why they lost or won a certain game by such a huge margin. Keep this analogy always in mind, no matter how knowledgeable a student of the investment world you become. Sometimes in the stock market and investment world, there is no way that anyone can logically explain in the short-term, why particular events happen. Over the long haul, however, there are clearly discernible reasons why stock prices in general increase or decrease in value. Let's review some of them.

CORPORATE PROFITS (EARNINGS)

Since stocks represent a part ownership of a corporation, it makes logical sense that investors want to own the shares of profitable companies and also companies that are expected to be very profitable. The greater the profits or expected profits, the more likely the stocks of those corporations will increase in value. This does not necessarily mean that once a company's earnings increase, it's stock price will also increase. Sometimes it takes the market in general a while to recognize profitable companies. Eventually, the stocks of well-run companies will increase in market value. You can compare stock values to real estate values. Often buyers of residential real estate do not see the investment potential of purchasing a home in a particular area until it becomes obvious to everyone. With 20/20 hindsight, they wonder how on earth they did not see the investment potential in the first place—the signs were so "obvious." So it is with stocks. Stock prices, especially those of small, well-run companies with increasing profit margins, may remain stable for years before many investors realize their positive investment value. Similar to real estate investments, finding these kinds of stocks takes time, patience, an analytical mind and, of course, money.

INTEREST RATES

Stock prices in general are very sensitive to interest rate changes by the Federal Reserve Board (FRB). The Federal Reserve Board chairman is the most important person in the country with respect to how the financial markets are impacted by changes in interest rates. That is why so many investors, politicians and financial institutions try to anticipate what the Federal Reserve Board will do about interest rates.

TWO MAJOR COMPETITORS FOR INVESTORS' MONEY

There are two major competitors for investors' money—equity and debt investments. If short-term interest rates are increased by the Federal Reserve Board, then many investors put their money into money market securities and savings accounts. This occurs because of the higher investment returns that money market securities and savings accounts offer.

On the other hand, if the Federal Reserve Board decreases short-term interest rates, then money market securities and savings accounts will pay lower interest rates. Many investors then look to the equities market for greener pastures. There is a constant see-saw going on between equity and debt investments for investors' dollars. As your knowledge about the basics of equity and debt investments grows, you will become increasingly aware of the powerful impact Federal Reserve Board interest rate changes have on the market value of various investments and the economy.

EMOTIONS AND INVESTING

In the short-term, the emotional response of individual investors and money managers at various financial institutions can have a powerful affect on stock prices. This emotional response is due to various events in the economy, interest rate changes, the political atmosphere—both domestically and internationally—and other occurrences.

As a beginner, you may presume that it is individual investors and not the big money managers at pension funds, mutual funds and insurance companies that often overreact to current events, but the evidence seems to be that indeed the opposite is the case. Many individual investors, at least those with a knowledge of the basics and with some investment experience, usually invest for the long-term and accept the fluctuations and occasional volatility of the stock market. Institutional investors, although very knowledgeable, often make short-term decisions. The "problem" is that many of them operate under "constraints" that do not present themselves to the individual investor. These "constraints" should become clear to you even after one reading of *One Up On Wall Street* by Peter Lynch with John Rothchild and *Bogle on Mutual Funds* by John Bogle.

STOCK MARKET BAROMETERS OR INDEXES

There are several barometers that measure how the stock market is doing every day. They are called indexes. You may have heard of one or two. The most famous is called the Dow Jones Industrial Average—DJIA. The DJIA or the Dow, as it is most often called, comprises the stocks of thirty large companies. Most of the companies that make up the DJIA are very well known—such as McDonald's, IBM, Coca-Cola and Microsoft.

While the Dow is the most often quoted and most famous barometer of what is happening to stock prices, it is not the most accurate. Remember that the thirty companies that comprise the Dow are all major companies. What about the thousands of other companies that comprise the U.S. stock market? Most people who follow the stock market closely quote and use the Standard and Poor's 500 as their benchmark or barometer for how the stock market is doing on a day-to-day or year-to-year basis. The Standard and Poor's 500 Composite Stock Price Index is an index of 500 large well-established companies.

A more accurate barometer of the U.S. stock market than the S&P 500 is the Wilshire 5000. As yet, this index is not used nearly as often by investment professionals or money managers as is the Standard and Poor's 500. The most well-known and quoted index for how small company stocks are doing is the Russell 2000. There are other market indexes, but these are the ones you should become familiar with and monitor for now.

GENERAL CATEGORIES OF STOCKS

Just as football players come in all sizes, talents, potential abilities, weaknesses, ages and so on, it is likewise true that corporations come with various types of strengths, weaknesses, ages and potential abilities. It takes time, research and an analytical mind to discern clearly the strengths, weaknesses and investment potential of the various stocks that are publicly traded. For now, as a beginner, you should know the major categories of stocks. Later, as your knowledge and experience in investing grows, you can analyze more thoroughly these major categories. Many of the books recommended at the end of this chapter will help you tremendously in this endeavor.

AGGRESSIVE GROWTH STOCKS

These are the stocks of small to medium-sized companies that are expected to grow rapidly. These stocks can be expected to fluctuate in price more frequently than blue chip or growth stocks. Aggressive growth stocks pay little dividends. These stocks are invested in with the expectation of high capital gains. The Russell 2000 is an index that monitors the fluctuation in market value of aggressive growth stocks.

GROWTH STOCKS (BLUE CHIP STOCKS)

These are the stocks of major well-established companies that have a long history of earnings growth and dividend payments. Many of these companies are household names, such as IBM, McDonalds, General Electric, Coca-Cola and Proctor and Gamble. They are called "blue chip" because blue chips are more valuable than either red or white chips in the game of poker. "Blue Chip" stocks are often referred to as growth stocks and vice versa. The index that measures the price changes in these stocks is the S&P 500.

INCOME STOCKS

These are the stocks of companies that have a consistent record of paying dividends. They also offer some potential for capital gains. Generally, they fluctuate in market value less than either growth or aggressive growth stocks. Over the long-term, their total investment returns are usually less than either growth or aggressive growth stocks.

DEFENSIVE STOCKS

These are the stocks of companies that have traditionally maintained their value during economic recessions. Food, drug and, until recently, utility companies are examples of defensive stocks.

CYCLICAL STOCKS

These are the stocks of companies whose earnings or profits fluctuate in tandem with the economy. If the economy is expanding, the earnings of these companies usually expand and their stock prices generally increase. When the economy is in a recession, the profits and share prices of these companies usually declines.

SPECIALTY STOCKS

These are the stocks of specific industries, specific countries, specific sectors of the economy and so on. The amount of specialty type stocks has increased in the past twenty years as more and more investors focus on specific niches of the market.

SUMMARY

The stock market can be a very exciting and financially rewarding place to invest your money. Difficult as it may seem at first to understand, stocks represent an ownership position in a corporation. Most corporations are private. The shares of private corporations are not publicly traded. Only the stocks of public corporations are traded on the New York Stock Exchange (NYSE), the American Stock Exchange (AMEX), the National Association of Securities Dealers Automated Quotation System (NASDAQ) and other smaller exchanges. Every year many privately held corporations decide to go public. They offer their shares for purchase through an initial public offering, in order to expand their business and make greater profits.

Yes, it's true that the challenge of analyzing and buying the stocks or shares of publicly traded corporations is beyond the capacity of beginning investors. But with just a little time and effort spent reading some of the books recommended at the end of this chapter, you should find yourself able to decide if purchasing individual stocks is an intelligent course of action for you to take.

As a novice, you should start investing in stocks through stock mutual funds. You can do so with confidence and even with very little money. This is particularly true if you can initially invest through a qualified retirement plan—such as a 401K, 403B, IRA or Roth IRA. Two other strategies that will help you begin investing in stocks with confidence and with little money are index investing and dollar-cost-averaging. Both of these investment strategies are discussed in Chapter 8. Mutual funds are also reviewed in Chapter 8.

YOUR STOCK INVESTING GAME PLAN

- *Always remember that when you buy stocks directly, or indirectly through a mutual fund, you become a part owner of a public corporation.* Sometimes experienced investors forget or ignore this important fact.

- *Keep in mind the major reasons why stocks increase or decrease in market value over the long-term.* Over the long haul—ten years or more—it is the fundamentals about a company, especially earnings and management, that are the most crucial determinants of its stock price. In the short run, many other factors—such as greed, fear, impatience, the domestic and international political situation, interest rate changes by the Federal Reserve Board, irrational exuberance and unwarranted pessimism—can play powerful roles in a stock's market value.

- *If you plan to invest in individual stocks at some time in the future, you should join an investment club.* Before you even do that, you should read several books about stock market investing. You can easily find out about any investment clubs in your area by calling the National Association of Investors Corporation (NAIC) at (248) 583-6242. The charge to join the NAIC is minimal.

- *Become familiar with the terminology at the end of this chapter.* Do not try to remember all of these financial terms. Consult the terms as a reference from time to time.

- *Become more knowledgeable about stocks by reading the following books written by these specialty investment coaches:*

  ➢ *One Up On Wall Street* by Peter Lynch with John Rothchild. Once you have a clear idea of what stocks are, you should not only find this book easy to read, but also a great source of inspiration to believing that you can catch up in a very short time.

➢ *How To Buy Stocks* by Louis Engel and Henry Hecht. This book has gone through numerous reprintings since first published in 1953. It is a great introduction to understanding stocks. It has a couple of superb chapters on bonds.

➢ *Buying Stocks Without A Broker* by Charles Carlson. In this book, you are shown how to invest in stocks without buying through a broker. Carlson lists the companies that sell directly to the public without any commission or sales charge. You will find this an excellent method to begin your individual stock picking, even with very little money or experience. This method of investing in stocks will give you a great sense of the market and hopefully will prove financially rewarding.

➢ *The New Money Masters* by John Train. This book is a great source of easy reading on how many of today's greatest stock investors planned their strategies. Some of these strategies can be used by beginning investors.

➢ *Starting and Running a Profitable Investment Club* by Thomas O'Hara and Kenneth Janke, Sr. If you later decide to invest in individual stocks, then you should become a member of a local investment club.

If you want to buy any of these books, see the section at the end of this book for where you can mail order them.

STOCKS—TERMINOLOGY

Across The Board - An advance or decline in stock prices that affects most shares.

Advance-Decline (A-D) - The amount of stocks that advanced versus those that declined on a given day or other period. Just like the prior phrase, across-the-board, it is a method of describing what is happening in the stock market. If the Advance-Decline day-to-day fluctuations of the stock market develops a pattern, many investors and commentators interpret this as either a bullish or bearish sign. Many times, this Advance-Decline is expressed in numeric form such as "Advancers Outnumbered Declines by a ratio of 3 to 1."

Aggressive Growth Stocks - Stocks of companies that are expected to grow rapidly. They are often the stocks of young companies with estimated high earnings potential. Many technology stocks fit into this category. What are called Aggressive Growth Stocks do not pay any dividends. Instead the profits are ploughed back into the company in the hope of greater growth and higher profits later. Aggressive Growth Stocks can be volatile.

American Stock Exchange (AMEX) - Like the New York Stock Exchange (NYSE), the American Stock Exchange is located in Manhattan, in New York City's Wall Street district. It is the financial capital of this country. The stocks of small to medium sized companies are usually traded, that is purchased and sold, on the American Stock Exchange. The stocks of large companies are generally traded on the New York Stock Exchange.

Beneficial-Owner of Stocks - Investors rarely keep the paper certifying stock ownership. It is normally held by the brokerage house in "street name." The Beneficial Owner of the Stock is the investor, but for safety and convenience reasons, it is kept at the brokerage company.

Bid and Ask Price - The price a buyer is willing to pay or "Bid" for a security, such as stocks. The Ask Price is the price that it is offered for sale at.

Big Board - Another term for the New York Stock Exchange or NYSE.

Block of Stock - A trade of 10,000 or more shares of stock at one time.

Blue Chip Stocks - These are the stocks of high quality companies that have a long history of sustained earnings growth. The phrase "Blue Chip" comes from the game of poker. Blue Chips are the most valuable chips in a poker game.

Bull Market - A relatively long period of generally rising stock market prices.

Buy-And-Hold Strategy - A stock market investment strategy employed by many intelligent investors. They buy the stocks of quality companies and hold those shares for the long-term, unless they believe the fundamentals of the companies have deteriorated. These investors are usually not intimidated into selling because of the occasional volatility of the market. *One Up On Wall Street* by Peter Lynch will show you how one of the greatest stock market investors went about this strategy of buying and holding the stocks of good companies. *The New Money Masters* by John Train is also an excellent source for learning how other great stock market investors went about implementing this Buy-And-Hold Strategy.

Common Stocks - Sometimes stocks or shares will be referred to as Common Stocks. On occasion you may hear the words preferred stock. Common Stocks are the ordinary shares of a corporation. They represent an ownership right in a company. Nothing more. Preferred stock entitles the owner to dividend payments, just like bondholders. You should become knowledgeable about Common Stocks now. Later, you can read up on preferred stocks.

Counter-Cyclical (Or Defensive) Stocks - Stocks of companies that grow or at least maintain their level of earnings during a recession. Examples of Counter-Cyclical Stocks are food, entertainment and utility stocks.

Cyclical Stocks - Stocks whose price movements fluctuate in tandem with the general economy. When the economy is expanding Cyclical Stocks generally increase in market value. When the economy is in a downturn or recession, Cyclical Stocks usually show a decline in market value.

Dow-Jones Industrial Average (DJIA) - The DJIA, commonly called the DOW, is an index or barometer that tells us how the stock prices of thirty very large U.S. companies are doing every day. The DOW is by far the most often quoted barometer of the U.S. stock market. Since it only tells us about the price movement of thirty very large U.S. companies, it is not the most accurate barometer of the U.S. stock market. The Standard and Poor's 500 is a more accurate barometer of the U.S. stock market. Better yet and the most accurate of all is the Wilshire 5000. It is the correct index to use for measuring the price movement of U.S. stocks every day.

Earnings-Per-Share (EPS) - This is an investment term that you should read more about later. *One Up On Wall Street* by Peter Lynch is one superb source of this information. Earnings-Per-Share is the net income of a public corporation divided by the total number of shares outstanding. You certainly can gain satisfactory investment yardage without knowing much about Earnings-Per-Share. If later you want to take up the challenge of trying to achieve superior investment returns, then you certainly should become knowledgeable about Earnings-Per-Share (EPS).

Efficient Market Theory - A stock market theory that says stock prices reflect all known information and adjust immediately on new information. Because the market is so efficient, according to this theory, it is not possible for investors to consistently outperform the market averages, such as the Standard and Poor's 500. The market averages have been beaten. But it is not easy. As Dr. Benjamin Graham stated in *The Intelligent Investor*, achieving "superior results is harder than it looks." The U.S. Securities markets are very *efficient* or competitive over the long-term. They are often not *efficient* or competitive in the short-term.

Fundamental Analysis - A stock market selection theory that emphasizes the study of a company's earnings, balance sheet, company management, state of the economy and it's future earnings outlook. In *One Up On Wall Street* you will read about how one great investor put this principle into practice. You will also read about others who have done the same in *The New Money Masters* by John Train.

Growth Stocks - These are the stocks of companies that are expected to have above average increases in earnings. Growth Stock companies retain most of their profits and reinvest those profits in order to achieve greater earnings growth later. Growth Stocks are expected to be occasionally volatile. Investors in Growth Stocks expect high capital gains and very little dividends.

High-Tech Stocks - These are the stocks of computer, biotechnology and robotics companies. Enormous profits can be made very fast in High-Tech Stocks, but great losses can also occur. Many investors are putting all their investment dollars in High-Tech Stocks. The consequences can be financially disastrous.

Income Stocks - Stocks that have a history of paying large dividends. They are purchased by many retirees who still want to invest in stocks for some capital growth, but also want some current income from their investment portfolio to supplement their retirement income. Income Stock investors should only expect moderate capital gains. Utility stocks are an example of Income Stocks.

Initial Public Offering (IPO) - This is when a corporation offers its stocks for sale for the first time. Initial Public Offerings are sold in the primary market. You don't need to learn much about IPO's now.

Large-Cap Stocks - The stocks of corporations that are well financed. Most Large-Cap Stocks are household names and have been around for a long time. Examples of Large-Cap Stocks are IBM, General Motors, General Electric, Exxon, Microsoft and McDonalds. Large-Cap Stocks are generally considered growth stocks. "Cap" is the abbreviated form for capitalized.

Market Correction - A sharp drop in stock prices. It may occur on one day or over several weeks and months. Any one of several factors could be the cause of a Market Correction or several factors could be the reason. Sometimes investors cannot pinpoint the rationale for a severe market decline, like one that occurred in October 1987. Long-term stock market investors should not lose sleep over these Market Corrections.

Penny Stocks - Stocks that are priced to sell at $1 or less. They are traded in the Over-The-Counter market (OTC). A beginning investor should not purchase Penny Stocks. Possibly later when they are very knowledgeable about stocks and have read books on stock market investing.

Preferred Stock - A cross between a stock and a bond. It gives an investor ownership rights in a corporation, but it also gives it's owner a claim on a company's assets, before common stockholders, in the event the assets are liquidated. Preferred Stocks usually pay a fixed dividend. This is not an area of investing that you should learn about now.

Price/Earnings Ratio - The Price/Earnings Ratio is commonly called the P/E Ratio. This is a term that you need not be familiar with as a beginning investor. Later you should certainly learn more about its importance. The P/E Ratio of a stock is obtained by dividing the price of a stock by its earnings per share.

Secondary Market - After stocks are initially sold for the first time in the primary market they are then purchased and sold in the Secondary Market. Big institutional investors, such as mutual funds, insurance companies and pension funds, often trade stocks among each other in large quantities in the third market.

Small-Cap Stocks - In contrast to large-cap stocks, which are the stocks of large and well-established companies, Small-Cap or Small-Capitalized Stocks are shares of small and not so well-established companies. The Russell 2000 is an index that tells us how the stocks of Small Capitalized companies are doing each business day. The Standard and Poor's 500 is a barometer of the market value of large-cap stocks.

Standard and Poor's 500 (S&P 500) Stock Market Index - This is an index that is quoted regularly in the press and media. It tells us how the stocks of 500 large U.S. companies are doing everyday. You should become familiar not only with the S&P 500 Stock Market Index, but the other major indexes as well—such as the DJIA, Wilshire 5000 and Russell 2000.

Stockholders/Shareholders - Investors who own shares of a public or private corporation. They have voting rights in that corporation. There are two ways they can share in the financial success of a company. One is by receiving dividends and the other is through the stock's or share's increase in market value.

Stock Market - This is the Market where Stocks are bought and sold everyday. The three major stock exchanges in the U.S. are the New York Stock Exchange (NYSE), American Stock Exchange (AMEX) and the National-Over-The-Counter market, commonly called NASDAQ. There are also several regional stock exchanges.

Stock Split - A corporation may issue a two for one Stock Split. Each stockholder automatically receives another share. The market price of the stock automatically drops 50 % in value. You can also have a Reverse Stock Split. A person who owns 1000 shares of a corporation will, after a Reverse Stock Split, own only 500 shares. But the shares will have doubled in market value. It is not important that you know much about Stock Splits now.

Stock Symbol - These are abbreviated symbols used by the various stock exchanges and others to record stock prices in manageable form. Stocks that trade on the NYSE have two or three letters. Stocks which trade on the AMEX have three or four symbols. Stocks traded on NASDAQ have four or five symbols.

Stocks or Shares - Stocks or Shares represent an ownership right in a corporation. Owners of Stocks or Shares have voting rights in a corporation. Those voting rights can direct the course of a company. For example, the board of directors of a corporation could be fired and replaced if a majority of stockholders decide to do so. One Share of Stock equals one vote. A person who owns a thousand Shares has a thousand votes.

Technical Analysis - This is a method of forecasting stock prices by interpreting historic value, price patterns and by the use of various charts and graphs showing market trends. This method of forecasting stock prices is way beyond the knowledge level of beginning investors.

Value Line Investment Survey - Value Line Investment Survey should be one of your main sources of data on thousands of companies if you decide after a reading of *One Up On Wall Street* and possibly a few other books on stock market investing, to investigate buying individual stocks. It is available at most libraries and major bookstores.

CHAPTER
◆ 6 ◆

BONDS

Medium and Occasional Long Yardage Gainers

The stock market is not the only investment game in town. In fact, it is dwarfed by the bond market. The bond market does not generate the same kind of media coverage as the stock market for two reasons. First, the stock market is more exciting and the media usually goes after excitement over substance like bees after honey. Second, the big money is made in the stock market. Nobody gets on the Forbes 500 richest by investing in bonds. Many do so by investing in stocks. Over the long run, the stock market is usually more financially rewarding than the bond market. For some, the stock market has brought them financial ruin. Less frequently, the bond market has done the same. The bond market is a more important player than the stock market in fueling our capitalist system.

WHAT ARE BONDS?

The word "bond" that is so often used in the investment world is derived from the everyday meaning and usage of the term. It can have different meanings, depending on the context. For example, two people can say they have a close bond between each other. They would be understood to have a close personal friendship. In another context, it could mean something different. For example, when Senator Bob Dole, during the Presidential Election campaign of 1996, said hundreds of times that "I give you my word, I give you my bond" or "my word is my bond," he meant the word "bond" to be a promise.

BONDS ARE LOANS

It was from these two meanings and contexts that the word bond came to describe a particular financial transaction. When one party lent another money, they established a new relationship. They established a bond. The borrower promised to return the money at a particular time and pay the lender a specified amount of interest for the use of the money either at regular intervals or in one lump sum.

Not all loans today are called bonds. The word bond in the investment world is reserved for a specific kind of loan. In *Getting Started in Bonds*, author Michael Thomsett states that a bond is "A debt obligation issued by a corporation or other issuer promising to pay periodic interest and to return loaned capital upon maturity. Maturity occurs five or more years from the issue date." This is the definition of a bond in its strictest sense.

When the financial press or commentators refer to bonds, it has a much broader meaning than this definition provided by Michael Thomsett. The bond market also includes U.S. Treasury bills, U.S. Treasury notes, municipal notes and money market instruments among others. Bank savings accounts and certificates of deposit are not included, although they are debt investments.

There are four crucial concepts you need to grasp about investing through bonds. They are explained below.

BOND INVESTORS ARE MONEY LENDERS

While it may seem self-evident, it is critical for the beginner to realize that the bondholder is a lender. This is the first important concept to understand about debt investing. The most obvious example of this is an individual buying U.S. Treasuries. What actually has happened in such a financial transaction is that an individual has lent his or her money to the U.S. government. Even though the financial resources of the individual may be minuscule compared to the borrower, such as the U.S. government or a large corporation, it is important for the lender to investigate the creditworthiness of the borrower.

CREDITWORTHINESS OF BORROWERS

The second important concept to understand about bond investing is to know how creditworthy these borrowers are. There are several excellent sources that rate the creditworthiness of these borrowers. The most respected and well-known are: Standard & Poor's, Moody's and Fitch Investors Services. Each of these three big credit-rating companies has its own grading system.

	STANDARD & POOR'S	MOODY'S	FITCH
Highest Quality:	AAA	Aaa	AAA
	AA	Aa	AA
	A	A	A
Medium Quality:	BBB	Baa	BBB
	BB	Ba	BB
	B	B	B
Poor Quality:	CCC	Caa	CCC
	CC	Ca	CC
	C	C	C
Lowest Quality:	DDD	DDD	
	DD	DD	
	D	D	

Bonds which are rated AAA, AA, A and BBB by both Standard & Poor's and Fitch and Aaa, Aa, A and Baa by Moody's are known as investment grade. The likelihood of the borrower defaulting on these bonds is very remote.

Bonds that are rated below investment grade by these three companies are called "junk" bonds. The lower the grade given to a bond, the greater the likelihood of default in the estimate of these three bond credit rating companies. The credit rating given a bond by these three companies is a major determinant of how much interest will be paid on the bond. Any rise or fall in this credit-rating after the bond is issued, will affect the bond's market value. This is just the beginning on the credit-rating of bonds.

IMPACT OF FRB INTEREST RATE CHANGES

The third important concept to understand about investing in bonds is how interest rate changes by the Federal Reserve Board affect the market value of existing bonds. This is the area of debt investing where the "London Fog" can rapidly roll in and a beginner can get confused easily. Consequently, they may think bonds are far more complex than they really are.

Federal Reserve Board (FRB) interest rate changes do not affect the interest rate received on existing bonds. Rather, they have a powerful impact on the buying and selling of existing bonds. Closely follow this next example and you'll see the importance of Federal Reserve Board interest rate changes.

An investor owns a twenty-year U.S. government bond that pays 6% annual interest and she wants to sell her bond. Let's say the Federal Reserve Board has increased interest rates several times since she purchased this bond. Who is going to offer her the amount that she paid for the bond? Certainly no one who knows the basics about bonds. Wouldn't it be foolish to buy her bond paying 6%, when for the same money a person can get a twenty-year U.S. government bond that now pays a higher interest rate than 6%? So, if she really wants to sell her bond, she must sell it below her cost or at a discount and suffer a capital loss.

Conversely, the opposite of this scenario is also true. If the Federal Reserve Board has decreased interest rates several times since she bought her twenty-year U.S. government bond, she can now sell it for more than she paid for it or at a premium. Why? Because if a bond buyer goes directly to the U.S. government, he or she can get only a twenty-year U.S.

government bond paying less than 6%. In this situation the bond owner or bondholder can make a profit or capital gain.

You now know the third most important concept about bond investing: when the Federal Reserve Board decreases interest rates, existing bonds increase in market value and when the Federal Reserve Board increases interest rates, existing bonds decrease in market value. Make sure you understand how Federal Reserve Board interest rate changes affect the market value of bonds and other debt investments before reading any more advanced material.

BOND CALLABILITY

The fourth concept you should know about bonds is "callability." Some bonds have this feature. It means that the issuer of the bond can redeem the bond before its maturity date. This scenario can be a financial problem. Here's why. If interest rates decline sharply, the bonds that have a "callable" feature as part of the contract will be redeemed by the issuer. Some bonds have a clause that states that the issuer cannot "call" or redeem the bond before a certain date. The investor or bond buyer whose monies or principal has been returned now faces the challenge of buying another bond with a similar interest rate. This is not likely to happen in our scenario because interest rates have fallen sharply. This phenomenon is known as the "opportunity cost of investing" because the bond has been called or redeemed and interest rates have fallen sharply. The investor, in this scenario, has lost the opportunity of investing in another bond offering the same terms.

THREE MAJOR TYPES OF BONDS

U.S. GOVERNMENT AND U.S. GOVERNMENT AGENCY BONDS

The United States government and semi or quasi government agencies are by far the biggest borrowers in the world. The U.S. government borrows trillions of dollars to finance the national debt by issuing three types of bonds: U.S. Treasury bills, U.S. Treasury notes and U.S. Treasury bonds. Various U.S. government agencies also borrow billions of dollars.

TREASURY BILLS

U.S. Treasury bills are short-term (twenty-six weeks or less) debt securities. They are offered for sale by the U.S. Treasury with thirteen and twenty-six week maturity dates. They are sold at a discount. A $10,000 U.S. Treasury bill is always purchased for less than $10,000. The Treasury pays $10,000 at maturity. The difference between what the buyer pays and what the U.S. Treasury pays back at maturity is the interest earned.

TREASURY NOTES

U.S. Treasury debt securities have maturity dates between two to ten years. While U.S. Treasury bills have a minimum offer of $10,000, a person can purchase a U.S. Treasury note for $1,000 or more. Unlike U.S. Treasury bills, Treasury notes are not sold at a discount but are said to be sold at face value.

TREASURY BONDS

These are also U.S. Treasury debt securities. They have a maturity date of any length greater than ten years. One can purchase a U.S. Treasury bond for as little as $1,000.

There are several ways to buy U.S. Treasury debt securities. A person can buy them directly from the U.S. Treasury in the primary market and he or she can buy already issued Treasury securities in the secondary market. U.S. Treasury securities are both the most liquid and most marketable securities in the world. That means that there is always an abundance of buyers and sellers of U.S. Treasury securities.

U.S. GOVERNMENT AGENCY BONDS

These are bonds that are issued by various agencies of the U.S. government.

Although there are many government agency bonds, the three you are likely to hear about most often in the media and financial press go by the names of Ginnie Mae, Fannie Mae and Freddie Mac. Ginnie Mae (GNMA) is the acronym for Government National Mortgage Association. Fannie Mae (FNMA) is the acronym for Federal National Mortgage Association and Freddie Mac (FHLB) is the acronym for Federal Home Loan Bank.

MUNICIPAL BONDS

Like the U.S. government, state and local governments, school districts and various other government agencies, borrow vast sums of money to finance a myriad of projects. They borrow this money by issuing bonds for certain time periods. You will often hear these bonds referred to as "munis." If you take any interest at all in state and local government politics, you will hear and read about numerous municipal bonds. For example, state politicians may talk about floating prison construction bonds or state highway construction bonds. The school district may discuss the idea of the voters passing a school construction bond. Cities issue bonds all the time for specific projects that benefit the local citizenry.

SPECIAL TAX STATUS OF MUNICIPAL BONDS

Municipal bonds enjoy special tax exempt status. Municipal bond interest income is free from federal income taxation, just as interest paid on U.S. Treasury bills, bonds and notes is exempt from state income taxes. Municipal bond interest is also exempt from state income taxes for bond owners who reside in the state that issued their bonds. Municipal bond interest is not exempt from state income taxation for those who own these bonds but reside in a state other than the one that issued the bond. For example, residents of New Jersey are not tax exempt on the interest income they receive from any California municipal bonds they own. They would be exempt if the bonds were New Jersey municipals. So when you hear the phrase, "buy Double-Tax-Free municipal bonds," it means that the interest earned is exempt from federal income taxation and state income taxation for residents of the state that issue the bonds.

CORPORATE BONDS

Corporations of all kinds issue bonds. They issue bonds in order to borrow money to finance some kind of expansion or business project. Just like municipal and U.S. government bonds, a corporation's creditworthiness is rated by the three major credit rating companies—Standard & Poor's, Moody's and Fitch Investor Services.

SUMMARY

What you have read is just a brief introduction to the world of bond (or debt) investing. The major borrowers that you should become familiar with are the U.S. federal government and federal government agencies, state and local municipalities and corporations. You should first establish how creditworthy these borrowers are. The three major companies that supply investors with credit-ratings of these borrowers are Standard & Poor's, Moody's and Fitch Investor Services. As a general principle, the higher the credit rating, the lower the amount of interest paid. The lower the credit rating, the higher the amount of interest paid. This is just a guideline. Other factors will also determine the amount of interest paid.

You should also become familiar with the effect Federal Reserve Board interest rate changes have on the market value of existing bonds. When the Federal Reserve Board increases interest rates, the market value of existing bonds declines. Conversly, when the Federal Reserve reduces interest rates, the market value of existing bonds increases. Most people are familiar with the specific interest rates banks and savings and loan organizations give on a regular passbook savings account or a certificate of deposit. A very important difference between bank certificates of deposit and bonds is the lack of a secondary market for CDs. In other words, certificates of deposit are not tradeable. There is no ready market of buyers and sellers. It is because of this ready market of millions of buyers and sellers that Federal Reserve Board interest rate changes plays such a critical role in the market value of bonds.

Before you read further on bonds, make sure you understand clearly these two points:

● When people or financial institutions invest in bonds, they are investing in debt. That is, they are lending some entity their money for which they will get paid a specified interest rate over a specific period of time.

● Federal Reserve Board interest rate changes affect the market value of bonds.

Keep these two all-important points in mind and you will likely find that the two books I've recommended will guide you to a greater understanding of this potentially important player in your investment game plan.

YOUR BOND INVESTING GAME PLAN

♦ *The first concept you should clearly understand about bonds is that the lender or investor is investing in debt.* The investor is lending his or her money to the bond issuer or borrower. You will often hear the phrase that bonds are IOU's. This simply means that I—the borrower—owe you the lender or IOU.

♦ *There are three additional concepts you should be aware of with respect to bond investing:*

> ➢ How creditworthy is the borrower or bond issuer?
> ➢ How Federal Reserve Board interest rate changes affect the market value of existing bonds. The rule to remember is this: when the Federal Reserve Board reduces short-term interest rates, existing bonds increase in market value, and when the Federal Reserve Board raises short-term interest rates, the market value of existing bonds decreases.
> ➢ Is a bond "callable?"

The bond prospectus always states whether a bond is "callable" or not and whether there is a specified period before it can be "called."

♦ *Become familiar with the bond market terminology at the end of this chapter.* It is quite extensive, so take your time. Once you begin to master most of this terminology, you are likely to find that this part of the investment world is not as complex as you may now assume.

♦ *If you decide to invest in bonds, do so initially through a bond mutual fund.* Later, as your investment knowledge of bonds increases, you certainly may consider investing in individual bonds.

♦ *Continue reading about bonds.* The following are both superb books for gaining more knowledge about this important investment player:

➢ *The Bond Book* by Annette Thau.

This book does more than cover the basics about bonds. Therefore, take your time to absorb the information it contains.

➢ Chapter 5 titled "How To Select a Bond Mutual Fund" in *Bogle On Mutual Funds*. Do not invest in bonds before you have read this chapter of Bogle's book. *Bogle On Mutual Funds* is also recommended in the chapter on mutual funds.

Again, refer to the section at the end of this book to see where you can mail order these recommended books.

BONDS—TERMINOLOGY

Accrual Bonds - These are bonds that do not pay interest periodically. Rather they accumulate interest which is paid at maturity. A zero coupon bond is an example of an Accrual Bond.

Accrued Interest - Interest that has accumulated since the last payment, but has not been paid out.

Active Bonds - Bonds that trade frequently and in high volume. Because they trade frequently, there is obviously a great demand for them.

After Tax Basis – Refers to the amount a bond will yield after taxation. Its return before taxation and any charges, such as commissions, is called the "total return."

At Par - A term used in bond trading that means a bond is selling for its face value. If a bond falls in price or market value and is then sold, it is traded at a discount. If its market value has increased it can be traded or sold at a premium.

Basis Point - The smallest measure used in quoting bond prices. One Basis Point is equal to .01% of the bond's yield. For example, if a bond's yield has changed from 8.60% to 9.60%, then it has changed 100 Basis Points. As you become familiar with bonds and bond terminology, you will have no difficulty remembering what a Basis Point is.

Bond - A debt security. Bonds are sold in specific denominations for a specified period of time. Bonds are issued by corporations, governments and government agencies. Bonds may be collateralized or unsecured. If sold unsecured, they are called debentures. Bond issuers are rated for creditworthiness by Standard and Poor's, Moody's and Fitch Investor Services. The amount of interest a bond pays depends on market conditions, how long the bond is issued for and the creditworthiness of the issuer, among other factors. Unlike certificates of deposit, which only earn interest, Bonds can earn capital gains, if they are sold above the amount they were purchased for. Bonds can also be sold at a loss. This would cause the bondholder to suffer a capital loss. When you invest in a Bond you are investing in debt. You are a lender and the government, government agency or corporation is the borrower. Bond basics are not complicated, so don't let the unfamiliar terminology throw you off.

Bondholder - An investor who has legal title to a government or corporate bond. The investor is a creditor. He or she has lent his or her money to the bond issuer. The bond issuer is a debtor or borrower. Bondholders are legally entitled to receive interest and have their principal returned at the bond's maturity date.

Bond Ratings - Bonds are rated for creditworthiness by Standard and Poor's, Moody's and Fitch Investor Services. Become familiar with how these credit rating companies grade bonds. AAA is the highest grade offered and it means the likelihood of the bond issuer defaulting on the interest and principal is remote. The lower the letter grading, such as a C or D, means the bond issuer is more likely to default on the interest and principal. Lower grade bonds pay a higher interest rate to compensate for this greater likelihood of defaulting on interest and principal.

Bond Total Return – Refers to a bond's interest payment plus or minus any capital gains or losses, without consideration for any sales charges or other expenses.

Callable Bond - A Callable Bond can be redeemed or paid off before it's maturity date. If a bond is "callable," it will be stated in the prospectus. This is very important for an investor to know. Here's why: a bond issuer will "call" a bond if interest rates have dropped significantly and they can issue a new bond that pays a lower interest rate. The investor is then confronted with the challenge of finding another bond that pays interest at the rate of the old bond. Not likely, since interest rates have fallen. Not all bonds have this "callable" feature. It is important, even for beginning investors, to be familiar with this term. The prospectus states that a certain period must elapse before a bond is "callable." This is known as "call protection."

Corporate Bond - It is a debt security issued by a corporation. Corporate Bonds are issued for different time periods. The interest paid on these bonds varies. Market conditions and the creditworthiness of the corporation in the estimation of Standard and Poor's and Moody's play critical roles in determining the interest paid.

Current Market Value of Bonds – Regardless of Federal Reserve Board interest rate changes, certificates of deposit at savings and loans do not fluctuate in market value because they are not tradeable. Bonds are tradeable. There are hundreds of thousands of buyers and sellers in the bond market every business day. The Market Value of Bonds change constantly.

Debenture - An unsecured bond. Such a bond is issued without collateral in the event of default on interest and principal. U.S. government securities offer no collateral. They are said to be issued on the "full faith and credit" of the government. All U.S. government securities have Standard and Poor's and Moody's top credit rating.

Federal National Mortgage Association (FNMA) - Commonly known as Fannie Mae. It is a private company that buys mortgages issued by other companies. FNMA packages these loans and sells them as securities. Many private and institutional investors invest in Fannie Mae securities.

Fixed Income Securities - Bonds are classified as Fixed Income Securities. U.S. government, state and local governments and corporations pay a fixed interest rate on their bonds. Although the interest payments are fixed, the market value of these bonds can and usually does fluctuate.

Government National Mortgage Association (GNMA) - Commonly called Ginnie Mae. This is a U.S. government owned corporation that buys, like Fannie Mae, mortgage loans and then packages these loans and sells them as debt securities. Mutual fund bond managers are very familiar with both Fannie Mae and Ginnie Mae securities.

Investment Grade Bonds - Any bonds that are rated BBB or better by Standard and Poor's and Baa or better by Moody's are considered Investment Grade Bonds. The likelihood of the issuer defaulting on the interest and principal payments of these bonds is much less than bonds with a lower grading.

Junk Bonds - Any bonds rated BB or below by Standard and Poor's or Ba by Moody's are classified as Junk Bonds. Since they carry a higher likelihood of default than investment grade bonds, they typically pay higher interest rates. Junk Bonds can play an intelligent role in some investors portfolios. Beginning investors should only buy investment grade bonds and then only through a bond mutual fund. Later, when they gain more knowledge about bonds, they can investigate the possibility of investing intelligently in Junk Bonds.

Municipal Bond Insurance - Many municipal bonds are insured against default or failure to pay interest and principal when due. The major reason state agencies secure Municipal Bond Insurance is to make their bonds more attractive to investors. Two major Municipal Bond Insurance companies are AMBAC indemnity company and the Municipal Bond Insurance Association (MBIA).

Municipal Bonds - Commonly called "munis." These are bonds issued by state and local governments and various other government agencies—such as school districts. Interest income from state municipal bonds is exempt from state income taxation to residents of the state who own them and it is also exempt from federal income taxation. The expression, "buy double-tax-free state municipal bonds" refers to this tax exemption on interest income from municipal bonds. Any capital gains achieved by investing in municipal bonds are not exempt from taxation at the federal or state level.

Notes - A U.S. government bond that matures between two and ten years. State municipal Notes mature in a little less time than U.S. government Notes.

Par Value - Also called a bond's "face value." It is the amount paid for a bond when first issued. Later, it can be sold at face or Par Value, at a discount or at a premium. When a bond is sold at a discount, it is sold for less than its Par Value. When sold at a premium, it is sold for more than its Par Value.

Premium Bond - This is a bond that has a market value greater than it's face value. It can be sold at a profit. A discount bond is one that has a market value less than its face value and if then sold, it is sold at a loss.

Series EE Bonds - U.S. government bonds which are issued at a deep discount—at one-half par value. They are available for purchase in various denominations from $50 to $10,000. When redeemed at maturity the bondholder is paid the bond's par value. The difference between its par value and initial purchase price is the interest earned.

Series HH Bonds - These are also U.S. government bonds, but they can only be purchased by exchanging Series EE bonds that have a market value of $500 or more. They mature in ten years. Interest is paid on them semiannually.

Short-Term Debt Securities - Debt securities of one year or less in duration. Examples are U.S. Treasury bills, commercial paper and bankers acceptances. It is usually called "the money market."

Tax-Exempt Bonds - These are state municipal bonds that are not only exempt from federal income taxes on their interest earnings, but are also exempt from state income taxation on their interest earnings, for residents of the state who own them. Tax Exempt Bonds have a strong appeal to many high income tax investors. Any capital gains achieved on these bonds are not tax exempt.

Yield - The interest earned on a bond. It is generally stated as a percentage of the market price.

Zero Coupon Bond - A bond that is bought at a deep discount from its face value. It does not pay interest regularly. Instead the interest is added to the principal semiannually and paid out at maturity.

CHAPTER
◆ 7 ◆

MONEY MARKET SECURITIES AND SAVINGS ACCOUNTS

Short Yardage Gainers

MARS AND VENUS IN INVESTING

Pick up any investment or financial planning book and invariably you'll find chapters titled "Stocks," "Bonds," "Mutual Funds," and "Savings Accounts," but you can be certain you are not likely to find one with a title as, "Money Market Securities and Savings Accounts." Certainly I haven't, and I've combed through the personal finance and investment section of many bookstores and libraries. Regularly, you'll find a chapter called "Savings Accounts." Sometimes you'll find a chapter heading titled "Money Market Mutual Funds." It's as if financial writers and commentators are operating on the same theory with respect to savings accounts and money market securities as the best-selling author Dr. John

Gray is with regards to men and women—that they are from two different planets.

It is amazing that most financial writers and commentators today treat traditional savings accounts and money market securities as two very different investment players. This is even more astounding in light of the fact that money market securities are now readily available as an investment vehicle for just about everyone through the medium of money market mutual funds and money market deposit accounts.

MONEY MARKET AND SAVINGS ACCOUNTS—MUCH IN COMMON

It is unfortunate that money market securities and savings accounts are not written about or discussed in the same chapter in investing books. If this happened, we would take a giant leap forward. Traditional savings accounts and money market securities have far more in common than "penny" and "blue chip" stocks. Yet, it is not at all unusual for both "penny" and "blue chip" stocks to be written about in a chapter on stocks. In fact, savings accounts and money market securities are far similar than "short-term" versus "long-term" bonds, yet both types of bonds will automatically be included in a chapter titled "Bonds."

Let's now examine traditional savings accounts and money market securities and you'll begin to see their differences and similarities. In so doing, you'll be in a better position to make more intelligent investment decisions, taking into account your financial circumstances, the current and expected future market conditions and your investment goals.

SAVINGS ACCOUNTS AND MONEY MARKET SECURITIES ARE INVESTMENTS

Incidentally, I've included both traditional savings accounts and money market securities under investing. Both savings accounts and money market securities fall inside my definition of an investment. Both are invested in with the expectation of gaining a greater financial return than the original invested principal, sometime in the future.

MONEY MARKET SECURITIES

It is very likely that most people do not know what money market securities are. The majority of people have seen and heard the words the money market or money market securities many times, but like so many other words and phrases from the investment world, they did not seem to have any relevance to their lives. This is regrettable, not only because it is easy to understand what money market securities are, but also because of the intelligent role Money Market Securities could play in the financial lives of some investors. Today, millions of people invest billions of dollars in traditional savings accounts and certificates of deposit, but if they knew the basics about money market securities, they could easily see that if they had some or most of those monies invested through this player, they could be investing more intelligently and maybe with greater investment rewards.

WHAT ARE MONEY MARKET SECURITIES?

Money market securities are debt security investments that mature in one year or less. Regular savings accounts and certificates of deposit under $100,000 are not now considered part of the money market. An important characteristic of any security is that it can be traded. The following are the most common money market securities:

U.S. TREASURY BILLS

U.S. Treasury bills are short-term debt securities issued by the U.S. Treasury. They can be purchased directly from the U.S. Treasury without any sales or administration charge, for periods of three to six months. The minimum amount of purchase is $10,000. It actually is a little less. Here's why—U.S. Treasury bills are said to be sold on a discounted basis. They are sold for less than their face value. The difference between what an investor pays and the face value of the Treasury bill is the interest earned. Simply put, when an investor buys a U.S. Treasury bill, he or she, as with

99

any debt investment, is lending money for a specified period of time and earning a certain amount of interest for doing so.

$10,000 is too high a threshold for many individuals but they can purchase U.S. Treasury bills indirectly, in smaller amounts, through money market mutual funds and money market deposit accounts. We will discuss these later in the chapter. U.S. Treasury bills offer the highest degree of principal safety of any investment, even higher than an FDIC (Federal Deposit Insurance Corporation) savings account or certificate of deposit. Even though U.S. Treasury bills are not collateralized, they still are rated the safest security in terms of principal, by the two most highly regarded credit rating companies—Standard & Poor's and Moody's. In fact, all U.S. government debt securities have Standard & Poor's and Moody's top credit rating.

COMMERCIAL PAPER (CP)

Commercial paper is a debt security issued by corporations. The minimum amount is $50,000. Commercial paper is an unsecured promissory note. In other words, the corporation does not offer any collateral if it defaults on paying the note or loan. Typical maturity times are thirty, sixty and ninety days, but can be as long as 270 days. Corporations that issue commercial paper are rated for creditworthiness by Standard & Poor's and Moody's.

Large financial institutions and mutual funds purchase commercial paper directly. Smaller investors can invest in commercial paper through money market deposit accounts and money market mutual funds. Commercial paper is given a number grade from 1 to 4 by both Standard & Poor's and Moody's, rather than the typical letter grading given to corporate, government and municipal bonds. A rating of 1 is the safest or has the highest credit rating and a rating of 4 is the least creditworthy or the most likely in their estimation to default.

Just as individuals may need a loan for a short-term financial transaction, so do many corporations. Commercial paper is the financial instrument used by corporations to transact this type of loan. Generally, commercial paper will pay a little higher interest rate than bank savings accounts or certificates of deposit. This traditional slightly higher rate of return could play an important part in the financial lives of many retirees who for a number of reasons do not want to invest in stocks or stock mutual funds.

BANKERS ACCEPTANCES (BA)

Banker's acceptances are debt securities issued by banks in order to finance trade and pay for merchandise. Usually, the trade is foreign. A typical scenario is as follows: a U.S. business wants to buy foreign produce or merchandise to sell domestically. The foreign producer or manufacturer wants to be paid immediately. To facilitate this transaction, the U.S. business will negotiate with a domestic bank, based on its creditworthiness, to have the bank pay the foreign producer or manufacturer. In turn, the U.S. business will repay the bank with interest over a certain negotiated period of time. The usual period is three months, but it could be as long as 270 days. Bankers acceptances are generally issued in amounts from one-half to one million dollars. The bank may at any time decide to sell the note or debt to another investor on a discounted basis, because it may want to use the money for some other project.

Small investors can invest in banker's acceptances through money market mutual funds and money market deposit accounts. Banker's acceptances, like commercial paper, usually pay a little higher interest rate than most certificates of deposit and traditional savings accounts.

REPURCHASE AGREEMENTS (REPOS)

A repurchase agreement is an agreement by a seller to buy back, at a later date, securities that have been sold. The buyer of the securities, for this temporary time period, is paid a negotiated interest rate. The typical securities in this type of investment transaction are U.S. Treasury and government agency securities, banker's acceptances, jumbo certificates of deposit and commercial paper. The securities act as collateral.

Repurchase agreements (REPOS) are beyond the financial capacity and sophistication of most investors to participate in directly, but they can do so with confidence through money market deposit accounts and money market mutual funds. Investors should have confidence in the ability of money market managers to make such purchases. The usually slightly higher yields, particularly from no-load money market mutual funds vis-à-vis traditional savings accounts or certificates of deposit, can be of great importance to certain individuals, especially retirees.

JUMBO CERTIFICATES OF DEPOSIT

Jumbo certificates of deposit are issued in denominations of $100,000 or more. They are therefore beyond the capacity of the average person to invest in directly. Similar to the other money market securities already discussed, a person can invest in jumbo certificates of deposit through money market deposit accounts and money market mutual funds. Unlike traditional certificates of deposit at local savings and loans and banks, jumbo certificates of deposit are easily tradeable. The market is said to be very liquid for this investment as it is for all other money market securities.

MONEY MARKET MUTUAL FUNDS (MMMF) and MONEY MARKET DEPOSIT ACCOUNTS (MMDA)

Without money market mutual funds (MMMF) and money market deposit accounts (MMDA), money market securities would be off limits to most people. The sums of money necessary to invest directly in money market securities is way beyond the financial capacity of most individuals. But now, thanks to these two relatively new investment products—money market mutual funds and money market deposit accounts—most people can invest indirectly in money market securities.

Money market mutual funds are run by mutual fund families, such as Fidelity, Dreyfus, Vanguard, T. Row Price and hundreds of others. Money market deposit accounts (MMDA) are offered by banks and savings and loan associations. Money market deposit accounts (MMDA's) are almost always FDIC (Federal Deposit Insurance Corporation) insured. Money market mutual funds (MMMF) are not. Money market mutual funds are insured by the Securities Investors Protection Corporation, commonly known as SIPC (pronounced "sipik"). Money market mutual funds usually offer a slightly higher yield than money market deposit accounts. This is particularly true in the case of no-load money market mutual funds.

SAVINGS ACCOUNTS

Today, there are a myriad of names for what we once called a savings account. Not many years ago, checking accounts paid no interest. Most do now. Typically, savings accounts are discussed separately from checking accounts but fundamentally they are the same. In opening a checking or savings account, all a person is basically doing is lending his or her money to the bank or savings and loan. The interest that can be earned in both types of accounts varies depending on many factors and the financial institutions.

The two major interest earning checking accounts are called NOW and super-NOW accounts. A super-NOW checking account pays a higher interest rate than a NOW account, but it also requires that a higher minimum balance be maintained in the account at all times. The minimum balance requirement for each account varies for each bank and savings and loan. Historically, the interest earned on both NOW and super-NOW checking accounts has been relatively low—generally lower than the inflation rate. So if you want an inflation hedge, you need to look at other investment players.

Most savings accounts don't offer much better. What are called passbook savings accounts may offer a little higher return than interest bearing checking accounts. In order to get a higher rate of interest than what is paid by NOW or super-NOW checking accounts, you must invest in certificates of deposit (CDs). Let's review briefly, the major types of savings accounts.

PASSBOOK SAVINGS ACCOUNTS

Passbook savings accounts usually pay a little higher interest rate than interest bearing checking accounts. Withdrawals can be made from these accounts at any time without penalty. Virtually all passbook savings accounts are FDIC insured. Historically, the interest paid on passbook savings accounts has been less than the inflation rate.

CERTIFICATES OF DEPOSIT (CDS)

Certificates of deposit are the most common form of savings account at most banks and savings and loans. Money is deposited in a certificate of deposit (CD) for an agreed-upon period of time, such as three, six, nine, twelve months or even longer. The amount of interest paid depends on the financial institution, the length of the CD, amount of money deposited and generally prevailing interest rates. If an investor withdraws any or all of the principal before the maturity date of the certificate of deposit (CD), there is a penalty charge that will significantly reduce the interest earned. If a CD is redeemed shortly after being opened, an investor can lose even a portion of the principal because of this penalty charge for early withdrawal or redemption. The interest rate paid on the typical certificate of deposit (CD) is usually a little higher than the inflation rate. Remember though that CD interest earnings are subject to income taxation. Therefore, the purchasing power of the invested dollar usually declines for most CD owners. Almost all CDs are FDIC insured and, therefore, offer an extremely high level of principal security. If it is important that the purchasing power of your invested dollar increase, at a level greater than the inflation rate and your income tax rate combined, then you should look to other investment players rather than bank savings accounts or certificates of deposit.

SUMMARY

Here are some principles you'll want to keep in mind about the short investment yardage gainers that we've covered in this chapter:

- Both money market securities and savings accounts are short-term debt investments of usually one year or less in duration.
- Bank CDs are sometimes purchased for longer than one year.
- Both of these investment players offer a high degree of principal security.
- Money market investments, such as U.S. Treasury bills, banker's acceptances, commercial paper, jumbo certificates of deposit and repurchase agreements are very liquid investments. They can easily be converted into cash without any loss of principal.
- There is always a huge volume of buyers and sellers willing to trade every business day in money market securities.
  Certificates of deposit can easily be cashed in. There is a penalty charge for early redemption. If a CD is liquidated shortly after being drawn up, an investor can lose a small portion of the principal.
- The interest earnings achieved by both of these debt investment players has only slightly exceeded the inflation rate since 1925. But when you take into account the taxation of interest earnings, inflation and acquisition costs, most people have seen the purchasing power of their invested dollars decline with money market securities and savings accounts.

YOUR MONEY MARKET AND SAVINGS ACCOUNT INVESTING GAME PLAN

Become familiar with the basics about each of these investments and try to see their important similarities and differences. Remember that they are short-term debt investments, usually of one year or less duration. They also offer a high degree of principal safety and liquidity.

Both of these investment players will be regularly touted as "almost risk free" by most financial writers and commentators. Clearly understand what they mean by "almost risk free."

Become familiar with the terminology at the end of this chapter. You should be able to master this brief and easy list of financial terms in a very short period of time.

Understand, from the outset, that investing in money market securities and savings accounts is not likely to increase the purchasing power of your invested dollars. There may be a short period or periods of time when there are exceptions to this rule. If, as you examine your current personal and financial situation and future financial goals, you realize that you need the purchasing power of your invested dollars to increase significantly over a long period of time, then you should look at other investment players. Those other players could be stocks, stock mutual funds and residential real estate.

Read Chapter 6 in Bogle on Mutual Funds by John Bogle. The chapter is titled "How to Select a Money Market Fund." The book—*Bogle on Mutual Funds* is also recommended in the next chapter on mutual funds. In addition, read pages 202–209 in *The Bond Book* by Annette Thau.

You can purchase these books by mail order. See the end of this book for ordering information.

MONEY MARKET SECURITIES AND SAVINGS ACCOUNTS—TERMINOLOGY

Annual Percentage Yield (APR) - The interest rate earned on an account that reflects the frequency of compounding. A savings account which compounds daily will produce a higher annual percentage yield than a savings account which compounds monthly.

Bankers Acceptances - Letters of credit offered by banks to finance commercial transactions between the delivery date of the products and the payment date. Bankers Acceptances are rated for creditworthiness. Usually they offer a very high degree of security of principal. They are short-term debt securities and are part of the money market.

Cash Equivalents - Also known as cash reserves or money market securities. These terms are often used interchangeably by the press, media and investment authors. Cash Equivalents are very liquid investments. In other words, they can easily be converted into cash without any loss of principal. They offer a high degree of principal security. Given the other investment players available, they are very poor in combating the terrible twins—taxes and inflation. The purchasing power of your invested dollars are unlikely to grow much, if at all, by investing in Cash Equivalents.

Certificate of Deposit (CDs) - A type of savings account offered by banks and savings and loans that pays a higher interest rate than passbook savings accounts. CDs require a minimum deposit and have maturities that can range anywhere from thirty-two days to eight years. There is an interest penalty if the CD is redeemed or cashed in before its stated maturity date. In comparing certificates of deposit, you should note the actual annual percentage yield, not just the rate of interest paid. In other words, check how often the interest is compounded. The same interest rate, if it is compounded daily, will yield a higher return than if it is compounded monthly or yearly.

Commercial Paper - A short-term unsecured promissory note issued by various corporations to finance short-term commercial transactions. Maturity can be anywhere from thirty to 270 days. Commercial Paper is rated for creditworthiness by Standard and Poor's and Moody's. Commercial Paper offers a high degree of principal security. It is part of the money market. Commercial Paper usually pays a little higher interest rate than certificates of deposit. Individual investors, including beginning investors, can easily invest with confidence in Commercial Paper through money market mutual funds and money market deposit accounts. Knowledgeable investors don't use the words Commercial Paper. They just simply say "Paper."

Compound Interest - The paying of interest on the principal plus the interest already earned. The shorter the period of compounding the greater the percentage yield. A savings account that pays 5% compounded daily will have a higher yield than a savings account which pays 5% that is compounded monthly.

Early Withdrawal Penalty - This is a charge or penalty made by banks and savings and loans for the early redemption on savings accounts, such as certificates of deposit. Because of the word "penalty," some people think this is an unfair charge. It is not. Investigate the amount of the Early Withdrawal Penalty on savings accounts. They vary.

Federal Deposit Insurance Corporation (FDIC) - This is an agency of the U.S. government which insures bank accounts up to $100,000 each. It is important to note that insurance is for each depositor at each bank, not each account. A person who has more than $100,000 at one bank should open another account at another bank for any monies over $100,000. If you are in this money category, inquire at your bank or savings and loan about FDIC rules.

Money Market Deposit Accounts (MMDA) - Money Market Deposit Accounts are offered by banks, credit unions and savings and loans. They invest in similar products as money market mutual funds—such as U.S. Treasury bills, bankers acceptances and commercial paper. Unlike money market mutual funds, Money Market Deposit Accounts are insured by the FDIC up to $100,000. Money Market Deposit Accounts usually pay a little higher interest than many certificates of deposit. Money Market Deposit Accounts generally pay a little lower interest rate than money market mutual funds—especially no-load money market mutual funds.

Money Market Mutual Funds (MMMF) - Mutual Funds that pool the monies of investors and then invests those monies in money market securities, such as U.S. Treasury bills, bankers acceptances and commercial paper. There is a chapter in *Bogle on Mutual Funds* by John Bogle on how to invest through Money Market Mutual Funds. You should read it. Money Market Mutual Funds are not FDIC insured.

Money Market Securities - The market for trading short-term debt securities. Money Market Securities mature in one year or less. Money Market Securities offer a high degree of principal security and are very liquid. Examples of Money Market Securities are U.S. Treasury bills, bankers acceptances and commercial paper. Beginning investors can easily invest with confidence in Money Market Securities through Money Market mutual funds and money market deposit accounts. Money Market Securities usually pay a little higher interest than comparable length savings accounts or certificates of deposit, particularly if the money is invested through no-load money market mutual funds.

National Credit Union Administration (NCUA) - An agency of the Federal government, similar to the FDIC, that insures accounts in all federal and many state chartered credit unions.

Passbook Savings Account - A small book issued by banks and savings and loans that issue savings accounts.

Savings Account - An account offered by banks and savings and loans that pays varying amounts of interest. The amount of interest paid depends on many factors, not the least of which is current prevailing market conditions. Although Savings Accounts are not usually considered investments by the general public, investment writers and commentators, there is actually no logical basis for this assumption. Why shouldn't traditional Savings Accounts be considered investments like government, municipal and corporate bonds and common stocks? This is a good example as to why investment writers and commentators make the investment world seem so much more complicated than it really is.

Savings Illusion - Many people who place their investment monies in traditional savings accounts and money market securities do not realize that the purchasing power of this money is usually declining, because of taxes and inflation. It is of course entirely possible that millions of people do realize that the purchasing power of their invested dollars are declining, but they know little about other investment players, particularly common stocks to do anything intelligent about it. Over and over, investment writers, financial commentators and other dispensers of advice will say or write that you cannot "lose" your money by placing it in FDIC insured savings accounts. That is true if the only meaningful definition of the word "lose" is the possibility of not getting back your principal. For most investors, a far more intelligent definition of the word "lose" is any loss in the purchasing power of their invested dollars. This definition of the word "lose" is so much more intelligent because compared to thirty years ago millions more people today are not only living longer but also are living many more years in retirement.

Share Draft Account - A form of checking account offered by credit unions. Interest is paid on this type of account. A minimum balance is required. The interest rate paid depends on the balance in the account, current market conditions and other factors.

CHAPTER
◆ 8 ◆

MUTUAL FUNDS

Short to Medium to Long Yardage Gainers

WHAT IS A MUTUAL FUND?

A mutual fund is a financial investment company that is set up according to the Investment Company Act of 1940. A mutual fund invests on behalf of people who share common goals, including individuals affiliated with financial institutions, employers, corporations and pension plans. Instead of buying individual stocks, bonds or other securities, a mutual fund investor buys a share of the mutual fund. This mutual fund share gives the investor partial ownership of a professionally selected portfolio of stocks, bonds or other securities. When you buy shares in a mutual fund, your money is pooled with that of other investors whose numbers may be in the thousands or hundreds of thousands. The mutual fund invests this money by purchasing various kinds of securities, depending on the fund's goals. These securities are carefully selected and managed to achieve the objectives of the fund.

MANY TYPES OF MUTUAL FUNDS

There are many types of mutual funds. Classification depends on each fund's organizational type, fee amounts and investment objectives. Answering some questions will help you classify any funds you may be considering.

HOW IS A MUTUAL FUND ORGANIZED?

First, you can understand mutual funds by dividing them into two major categories—either open-end or closed-end funds. A closed-end fund issues a set number of shares just once when it begins. After shares in the fund have all been purchased, they are traded in the secondary market.

The open-end fund predominates, so you should become familiar with this type of fund now. Later, you can look into closed-end mutual funds, a category best suited for experienced investors. In open-end funds, investors buy from and sell their shares back to the mutual fund itself.

WHAT ABOUT FEES?

The second major factor you should consider in classifying a mutual fund is whether the fund charges any fees for buying shares. The mutual fund prospectus spells out the sales charges, if any, for purchasing shares in the fund. It will tell you if it is a load fund, no-load fund or some combination thereof. A load fund charges a commission to buy shares. A no-load fund doesn't charge a commission to buy shares. Low-load funds typically charge about half the fee of load funds.

WHAT ARE THE FUND'S OBJECTIVES?

A third way you can classify mutual funds is by their investment objectives. There are now more mutual funds in existence (not mutual fund families, which we'll get to later) than the number of stocks traded on the New York Stock Exchange (NYSE). Yet we can still classify them into ten broad categories. The following paragraphs can help you become familiar with the marketplace terminology used to describe different kinds of funds according to their objectives.

1. MONEY MARKET MUTUAL FUNDS

Money market mutual funds are funds that invest exclusively in debt securities that mature within one year. Examples of these debt securities are U.S. Treasury bills, U.S. government agency securities, jumbo certificates of deposit, commercial paper and short-term corporate bonds of large U.S. corporations.

Money market funds provide a high degree of principal safety and liquidity. These funds usually pay a little higher interest rate than comparable length bank certificates of deposit. This is particularly true if the monies are invested through no-load money market funds. While this difference may not seem significant for young investors, it can be very important for many retirees, who feel they must have a high degree of principal safety and liquidity while earning a little higher interest rate than the average certificate of deposit (CD).

2. AGGRESSIVE GROWTH MUTUAL FUNDS

Aggressive growth mutual funds strive for maximum capital gains. These mutual funds purchase the stocks of companies they believe will rapidly increase in value. Typically, these purchases will be stocks of young companies. Since these stocks are purchased with the expectation of rapid growth, they can fluctuate significantly in value and could be volatile.

3. GROWTH MUTUAL FUNDS

Growth mutual funds try to achieve high capital gains. They usually invest in the stocks of established companies whose stocks do not usually increase or decline in market value as rapidly as the stocks of young companies. A person who invests in either aggressive growth or growth funds counts on high capital gains and little dividends.

4. GROWTH AND INCOME MUTUAL FUNDS

A mutual fund whose objective is both growth and also current income invests in the stocks of companies that have a good record of consistent dividend payments. An investor in a growth and income fund should expect moderate capital gains and current income.

5. INCOME MUTUAL FUNDS

The objective of an income mutual fund is to provide a high level of current dividend income. This type of fund invests in several types of income yielding securities, such as high yielding dividend paying stocks. As a rule, the higher your expectation of current income, the more likely you are to see a significant variability in the returns of the underlying securities .

6. BALANCED MUTUAL FUNDS

Balanced mutual funds invest in a combination of stocks and bonds. Ordinarily, balanced funds invest about 60 % of their money in large company stocks and approximately 40 % in top grade bonds. People who want their investments to yield moderate to high current income but also want to emphasize the safety of their principal may find that this kind of fund will help them meet their goals.

7. BOND AND PREFERRED STOCK MUTUAL FUNDS

These mutual funds invest in both bonds and preferred stocks, with an objective of high current income rather than growth. The funds that exclusively invest in bonds are, as you might expect, called bond funds. There are two basic types of bond funds: one typically invests in corporate bonds and the other invests in U.S. government and municipal bonds. In periods of volatile interest rates, bond funds are subject to significant fluctuations in market value.

8. INDEX MUTUAL FUNDS

Index mutual funds hold only the securities of a particular index, such as the Dow Jones Industrial Average (DJIA), Standard & Poor's 500 (S&P 500), the Russell 2000 and the Wilshire 5000. These funds try to perform exactly as the index performs. Index investing has dramatically increased in popularity in the past two decades. In *Bogle on Mutual Funds*, John

Bogle devotes a chapter to index investing. This is must reading for the beginning investor. *Index Your Way To Investment Success* by Walter Good and Roy Hermansen should also be on your "must read" list.

9. SECTOR MUTUAL FUNDS

Sector mutual funds specialize in specific types of companies and industries. Some invest in utility companies. Others invest in gold, precious metals, or government securities. There is now a vast array of very particular sector funds in which you can choose to invest.

10. INTERNATIONAL MUTUAL FUNDS

International mutual funds invest in the stocks and bonds of corporations trading on foreign exchanges. Some invest in the stocks and bonds of a particular world region. Others invest in specific countries. Some of these funds may include the stocks and bonds of U.S. companies. The variety of international funds has exploded in the last few decades.

FOUR IMPORTANT CHARACTERISTICS OF MUTUAL FUNDS

1. DIVERSIFICATION

Mutual funds generally offer a high degree of investment diversification. This level of diversification is beyond the reach of most people who purchase individual stocks, bonds or money market securities. For a small amount of money, often as low as $500 or $1,000, an investor can instantly reach the goal of diversification. These initial small investment amounts of $500 to $1,000 are available with most mutual fund families, particularly if the monies are invested inside a tax deferred account— such as a 401K, 403B, or regular IRA account.

Most financial advisors would agree that even a well-selected portfolio of individual stocks needs at least ten different types of stock selections in order to attain a reasonable degree of diversification. Mutual funds offer a superior way for people with modest incomes to acquire investment diversification in spite of their very limited financial resources.

2. PROFESSIONAL MANAGEMENT

Mutual funds are overseen by either an individual manager or a fund committee. These investment professionals strive to manage the fund in accordance with its objectives. It is their responsibility to keep track of the performance of the different securities within the fund. It's also their duty to buy and sell shares for the fund. Individual fund managers or management teams are assisted by a staff of analysts, researchers, secretaries, accountants and other support.

3. LIQUIDITY

Usually, mutual fund shares can be acquired and sold on very short notice. Mutual fund companies always stand ready to redeem shares in the fund. Although liquidating stocks or bonds is typically not a problem, it can be when there are few buyers in the market for "thinly traded issues" and when the markets are very volatile.

4. CONVENIENCE

Mutual fund investing has many conveniences that are not available with other types of investing. You'll find explanations of the chief conveniences in the paragraphs below.

- Automatic Reinvestment of Dividends and Capital Gains Distributions
- Instead of receiving any dividends or capital gains, you can elect to have your dividends and capital gains automatically reinvested in additional shares or even fractions of the fund's shares.
- Regular Additional Investments
  When you initially apply to purchase shares in a mutual fund, you can opt to have a specific amount withdrawn from your checking or savings account each month to purchase addi-

tional shares or even fractions of additional shares. This is
an excellent investment strategy for beginning and experienced investors alike to overcome the temptation and challenge of trying to time the market. This method of investing
is called dollar-cost-averaging.

♦ Systematic Withdrawals

You can request to have a certain amount of shares liquidated each month. This can be an excellent retirement strategy for those with limited liquid resources who need additional money to augment their Social Security income.

♦ Telephone Exchanges

Most mutual fund families will allow you to exchange shares
in one fund for shares in another fund in the same family of
funds via the telephone and often at no extra cost.

HOW DO YOU SELECT A MUTUAL FUND FOR INVESTING?

There are currently over 8,000 mutual funds in which you can invest. Many
families of funds offer more than sixty mutual funds from which you can
choose. With such a broad range of choices, where does one begin?

♦ Mutual Fund Prospectus

One place to start is with the mutual fund prospectus, a publication that reports on the fund's goals, investment activites
and track record. A mutual fund must send a prospectus
before they accept your monies to invest. Put off by the volume of data presented, most people barely scan the prospectus. Nevertheless, this document provides valuable information. Read through a prospectus completely at least once. You
can then examine it closely by reading the most important
sections, including the fund's objectives, its past performance
record and the minimum required investment amount. Other
features you'll find in this report include automatic reinvestment of dividends and capital gains in additional shares, tele-

phone exchange choices, sales charges, management and 12B-1 fees.

♦ Past Performance

An important factor in judging the likely future performance of a fund is its past performance. The two current major sources of this past performance data are Morningstar and Lipper Analytical Services. You will often see both of these investment data services cited in the major financial magazines and newspapers. You can check a fund's record by looking at a number of these readily available magazines that regularly publish data on past performances of key mutual funds. Useful magazines include *Money, Worth, Forbes* and *Business Week.*

You can find these financial magazines in most bookstores, newsstands and in the periodical section of your public library. You ought to regularly subscribe to at least one of them after you have mastered the basics in this book and become familiar and comfortable with the investment terminology at the end of most chapters. While past performance is no guarantee of future results, it certainly is a factor that an investor needs to seriously consider when comparing funds.

♦ The Fund Manager or Fund Committee

Review the past record of the mutual fund management. Most mutual funds are managed by one individual and his or her support staff. Some funds are managed by two or more people. Often, this is referred to as "management by committee." In order to assess a fund's reliability, you need to answer a number of question about the management. How long has the manager been handling the fund? What has been this manager's performance record? The major financial magazines we've talked about are good sources of information on fund managers.

● Your Investment Goals

What investment goals do you want to achieve? Are your goals intelligent in light of your circumstances, the current market and expected future market conditions? For what length of time are you investing? It is absolutely critical that you strive to answer these questions intelligently before investing. If your investment goal is to achieve high long-term capital gains, are you willing to tolerate market fluctuations and even occasional volatility? If, on the other hand, your investment strategy includes security of principal at all times, then are you willing to accept investment gains that are likely to be less than the rate of inflation and taxes combined?

● Fees, Charges and Commissions

How do mutual funds assess their various fees, charges and commissions? The prospectus spells out the fees, charges and commissions (if any) that the fund may collect. The financial magazines mentioned earlier, such as *Worth, Forbes, Money and Business Week*, consistently report and compare the various fees, charges and commissions. These costs are an important consideration in making wise investment choices. You should be aware of the following four major types of charges that mutual funds may assess.

1. Sales Charge, Commission or Load

   About half of all mutual funds charge some kind of sales load or commission. Typically, these are the companies with registered representatives, stockbrokers and financial planners who sell various companies' mutual fund shares. Many funds that use in-house staff to sell their shares do not charge a sales commission, or *load* as they are commonly called. Some mutual funds sell their shares directly to the public and charge a load. These are usually called *low-load* funds. These types of funds charge less than the full-service mutual fund.

2. Management Fees (also called Investment Advisory Fees)
   The management fee is a certain percentage of the money invested that is under management by the mutual fund. It can be as low as .2% or even as high as 5%. The typical range is between .5% and 2%. The prospectus states the amount of the annual management fee.

3. 12B-1 Fees
   According to a ruling made in 1980 by the United States Securities and Exchange Commission (SEC), a mutual fund can legally charge fees for marketing and distribution costs. Some mutual funds do not charge 12B-1 fees. If a fund does assess 12B-1 fees, this cost will appear in the prospectus.

4. Other Miscellaneous Fees
   The fund may assess an administration charge, typically about .2% to .4% of the monies invested. You may have to pay for custodial, state and local taxes, legal and audit expenses and director's fees.

Taxation Consequences

Knowing the basics about how the government taxes investment gains or losses is an important part of planning an intelligent investment plan. Capital gains, interest and dividend income from investments are subject to income taxation, unless specifically excluded or exempt by federal or state law—or both. One of the easiest and smartest ways to shield investment capital gains, dividends and interest earnings from current income taxation is to have them legally invested in a tax sheltered or tax deferred account. Examples of the most popular and frequently used tax sheltered or tax deferred investment accounts are 401K's,

403B's, IRA's, Roth IRA's, Variable Annuities, Variable Universal Life, Keogh Plans, SEPIRA Accounts, Fixed Life and Fixed Annuities.

◆ Mutual Fund Families

A mutual fund which offers two or more mutual funds that are administered by the same company is a mutual fund family. Many mutual fund families, such as Vanguard and Fidelity investments, offer more than sixty mutual funds through which you can invest. The funds have various investment objectives in order to meet the needs of the investing public. Mutual fund families offer benefits that are not available with a single fund company. The most useful option is the ability to move shares from one mutual fund into another mutual fund of the same family. This can be done usually over the telephone and often without any sales charge.

DOLLAR-COST-AVERAGING

Dollar-cost-averaging is a strategy whereby you invest the same amount of money at regular intervals in a mutual fund or other investment. While there are many advantages to pursuing a dollar-cost-averaging strategy, we cover the two most important ones below.

◆ You develop positive investment habits.

Given the fact that we are creatures of habit, it is essential that you develop a systematic investment strategy as soon as possible. On a regular basis, usually monthly, invest the same amount of money into your investment portfolio. Regardless of how compelling the reason might be to do otherwise, in the long run you will easily see the enormous positive value of investing a specific amount of money, month after month, without regard to current market conditions. Although this strategy may seem to fly in the face of logic, the evidence is overwhelming that investors who use a dollar-cost-averaging investment strategy are pursuing an intelligent investment game plan.

◆ You avoid second-guessing market fluctuations.

Dollar-cost-averaging can help you avoid the challenge of trying to time the market. The biggest market gains and declines are often concentrated in very short periods of time. Even experienced and disciplined investors find it extremely challenging to time the market accurately. This is why the amateur investor, with a basic knowledge of investing and a systematic plan of dollar-cost-averaging, sometimes surpasses the so-called professionals and sophisticated investors over long periods of time.

MUTUAL FUND INDEX INVESTING

Mutual fund index investing, a relatively new investment strategy, was introduced to the industry in 1971. An index mutual fund purchases the stocks, bonds or other securities that comprise a particular index. The popularity of indexing has skyrocketed during the past two decades.

The first public mutual fund index, pioneered by Vanguard Company in 1976, replicated the Standard and Poor's 500. As monies came into this fund, it purchased the stocks of the 500 companies listed in the Standard and Poor's 500. No research was involved. All Vanguard attempted to do was mimic the results of the Standard and Poor's 500. Of course, the fund charged investors a small fee for duplicating the market returns of the Standard and Poor's 500. Incidentally, the charges for index funds are usually much lower than for other mutual funds.

Today, you'll find many index mutual funds that you can choose to invest in. I've described the most well-known in the following paragraphs.

DOW JONES INDUSTRIAL AVERAGE (DJIA) INDEX FUND

Mutual funds of this type purchase the stocks that comprise the DJIA. These are the stocks of the thirty largest *blue chip* companies. Virtually everyone has heard of the DJIA, even though many have no idea what it really means. Anyone who invests in a DJIA index mutual fund should expect similar investment returns as the DJIA, minus any fund charges.

STANDARD AND POOR'S 500 (S&P 500) INDEX FUND

This type of mutual fund tries to replicate the returns of the Standard and Poor's 500. As monies flow into the fund, it purchases the stocks of companies that comprise the Standard and Poor's 500. As we've noted, index funds do not conduct any research. Anyone who invests in this type of mutual fund should expect returns similar to the Standard and Poor's 500, minus any fund charges.

RUSSELL 2000 INDEX FUND

In this case, the mutual fund tries to mirror the returns of the 2000 stocks that comprise the Russell 2000. The Russell 2000 is the barometer of how well or poorly small capitalized public companies are doing. The stocks that comprise the DJIA and the S&P 500 are shares of large capitalized companies. Think of the Russell 2000 as representing the stocks of relatively small companies, and the DJIA and S&P 500 as representing the stocks of large companies. Historically, the stocks of the Russell 2000 have fluctuated more than those of the DJIA and the S&P 500, but their returns have also been greater over the long run.

WILSHIRE 5000 INDEX FUND

Here, the mutual fund attempts to mimic the returns of the stocks that comprise the Wilshire 5000. The Wilshire 5000 is the most accurate barometer of the U.S. stock market. Although the DJIA is quoted thousands of times daily in the media as a barometer of the U.S. stock market, it is heavily skewed towards the very large companies Therefore, it is not as accurate as the Wilshire 5000 or even the Standard and Poor's 500.

LEHMAN BROTHERS AGGREGATE BOND INDEX FUND

Bond mutual fund index investing is an even more recent phenomenon than stock market mutual fund index investing. It too is gaining in popularity. The most popular bond type index fund simulates the Lehman Brothers Aggregate Bond Index. It is a composite bond index and similar to the Wilshire 5000 with respect to stocks. It includes virtually all investment grade bonds—that is bonds that are rated BBB or better by Standard and Poor's and Baa or better by Moody's.

SUMMARY

Compared to investment options of the not-too-distant past, mutual funds offer today's beginning investor an enviable opportunity to enter the world of investing with high confidence and low investment amounts. Many mutual funds will accept as little as $1,000 to buy shares in a fund, and even much less if invested inside a tax sheltered account, such as a 401K, 403B, IRA, Roth IRA, Keogh and SEP-IRA.

There are an endless variety of mutual funds from which you can choose to invest in. Many mutual fund families, such as Vanguard, Fidelity, Dreyfus, T. Row Price and several others, offer over sixty mutual funds, many of which can help you reach your investment goals. Large mutual fund families offer the investor a low-cost choice of buying and selling shares in one mutual fund for shares in another mutual fund of the same family. This option can help you meet any change in your investment strategy that you may need because of changes in personal circumstances or market conditions.

Index investing has made it easier for today's beginning investor to decide which mutual fund to invest through. Your source for your in-depth knowledge of index investing is Chapter 9, titled "Index Investing" in *Bogle On Mutual Funds*. John Bogle has been called the "king of indexing"—a well deserved title, for he has clearly shown that index investing is a very intelligent strategy for beginning and experienced investors alike.

YOUR MUTUAL FUND INVESTING GAME PLAN

⬤ *Become familiar with the basic principles and terms of mutual funds.* Once you know the basics about stocks, bonds and money market securities, you should find it relatively easy to understand the fundamentals about mutual funds. Consulting the terminology at the end of this chapter will help as you seek to understand mutual funds.

⬤ *Use dollar-cost-averaging.* If you decide to invest in one or several mutual funds, use dollar-cost-averaging to build up your investment portfolio. With dollar-cost-averaging, you will avoid the challenge of trying to time the market. You will also get into the very good habit of automatically investing a percentage of your income each month. As the excitement of the investment world takes hold of you, you will probably find it easier to increase the amount you invest every month by using this method.

⬤ *Automatically reinvest any dividends and capital gains by buying additional shares in the fund.* You can specify this option when you open your mutual fund account. Your investment portfolio will appreciate more rapidly through the use of this strategy.

⬤ *Strongly consider index investing as your first choice in mutual fund investing.* To help you decide which index to use, read Chapter 9 in *Bogle On Mutual Funds*. Later, as your knowledge and experience of investing grows, you may want to consider other options, but only after careful review. Also read *Index Your Way To Investment Success* by Walter Good and Roy Hermansen.

⬤ *Read* <u>Bogle On Mutual Funds</u> *and other essential books.* This book is likely to become an investment classic, similar to Benjamin Graham's *The Intelligent Investor.*

A section in the back of this book has a mail order offer to purchase the books discussed in this and other chapters.

MUTUAL FUNDS—TERMINOLOGY

12B-1 Fees - This is a fee charged by mutual funds for advertising and marketing. It varies from one mutual fund company to another. Some funds do not charge 12B-1 fees.

Aggressive Growth Fund - This is a mutual fund that invests in the stocks of young or even established companies that pay little to no dividends, but offer the possibility of high capital gains. An Aggressive Growth Fund is likely to experience more volatility than other mutual funds. Aggressive Growth Funds are very suitable for young investors who have a long-term investment horizon and who are also willing to accept the occasional volatility inherent in investing in these kinds of stocks.

Automatic Reinvestment Plan - This phrase applies to mutual funds that allow shareholders to automatically reinvest dividends, interest earnings and any capital gains in additional shares or fractions of shares of the mutual fund. Most investors specify this option when they complete the mutual fund application. It is an intelligent investment strategy.

Automatic Withdrawal - Most mutual funds allow an investor to set up an Automatic Withdrawal program. Often, retirees set up Automatic Withdrawals from their mutual funds to supplement their retirement program.

Back-End Load - Also known as a contingent deferred sales charge (CDSC). This is a fee charged by many mutual funds for redeeming shares in the fund before a previously specified period of time has elapsed. These contingent deferred sales charges disappear after a certain time period. CDSCs are made by mutual funds that use stockbrokers, financial planners and other agents to sell shares in their funds.

Balanced Mutual Fund - A mutual fund that invests in stocks and bonds. The goal of such a fund is to provide some current income as well as offer the potential for some capital gains.

The percentage split between stocks and bonds varies with each Balanced Mutual Fund.

Basis - In mutual fund investing, Basis means the cost of the shares plus any commissions or sales charges.

Bid Price/Ask Price - The Bid Price is the price at which a mutual fund will buy back or redeem shares. The Ask Price is the current Net Asset Value (NAV) per share, plus any sales charges. The Ask Price is often referred to as the "offer price."

Bond Mutual Fund - A mutual fund which invests solely in bonds. The range of Bond Mutual Funds is enormous. It is even larger than the range of stock funds. A Bond Fund, for example, may only invest in AAA municipal bonds of a particular state. You can invest—not that you should as a beginning investor—in a corporate junk Bond Fund. Just a basic familiarity with bonds will go a long way in helping you decide what kind of Bond Mutual Fund you should consider investing through.

Confirmation Statements - These are statements sent to customers by a mutual fund after the initial purchase of shares. They contain pertinent and easy-to-read information.

Exchange Privilege - A privilege or option with most mutual fund families. It allows an investor to exchange shares of one mutual fund for shares in another mutual fund in the same family of funds. This can be done usually without any sales charge. This is a great option to have in your investment program. Personal circumstances and market conditions can change, so a person should have the option of changing their investment strategy with minimal effort and cost.

Family of Funds - Any fund with two or more mutual funds under the same management company is called a Family of Funds. Many companies manage over sixty different mutual funds. Fidelity Investments, Vanguard, T. Roe Price, Dreyfus and Scudder Kemper are examples of companies that manage Families of Funds.

Front-End Load Fund - A mutual fund that charges a commission to buy shares of the fund. About half of all mutual funds make some kind of sales charge. Commission charges are separate from any management or other expense charges made by a mutual fund.

Growth and Income Mutual Fund - This type of fund, also called a balanced fund, invests in stocks and bonds in order to provide current income and the opportunity for some capital gains.

Growth Mutual Fund - A mutual fund which invests in the stocks of medium to large companies that have consistently recorded earnings growth. These kinds of funds offer the potential for high capital gains. A Growth Mutual Fund is an intelligent strategy for those with a long-term investment horizon and who are willing to stay the course, regardless of the usual ups and downs of the market.

Index Mutual Fund - This is a mutual fund that simply invests in the stocks and bonds that comprise a particular index. A stock Index Mutual Fund buys the stocks of a specific index, such as the Dow Jones Industrial Average, Standard and Poor's 500, Russell 2000 or Wilshire 5000. No research or analysis is involved. There are now several bond Index Mutual Funds. Index investing has become an extremely popular method of investing, especially during the past two decades. I cannot emphasize enough how important it is for beginning investors to investigate this strategy further by reading Chapter 9, "Index Funds," in *Bogle On Mutual Funds* and the book *Index Your Way To Investment Success* by Walter Good and Roy Hermansen.

International Mutual Fund - A mutual fund that invests in the stocks and bonds of other countries. The amount and different types of International Mutual Funds has risen dramatically in the past twenty years. International investing is subject to currency volatility. Beginning investors should invest first in U.S. securities before investing in international stocks and bonds.

Low-Load Mutual Funds - These are mutual funds that charge a lower commission, typically between 1% and 3%, than full commission funds, which average between 4% to 6% of the principal invested.

Management Fee - A mutual fund charges a fee for monies under management. Investors should thoroughly investigate the sales and Management Fee expenses a fund may assess.

Monthly Investment Plan (MIP) - Also known as dollar-cost-averaging. An investment strategy whereby a person routinely invests the same amount of money in, for example, a mutual fund. Most mutual funds allow automatic deduction of monies from a bank account to be applied to the purchase of shares in the fund. This can be a very intelligent investment strategy for beginning and experienced investors alike.

Mutual Fund - An investment company set up according to the Investment Company Act of 1940. In order to achieve the goals of the Mutual Fund, the company invests the monies of individuals, financial institutions, pension funds and retirement plans. Buying shares in a Mutual Fund gives an investor ownership rights in the fund. Mutual Funds offer advantages not found in other investments, such as the potential for investment diversification, small investment entry amount, automatic reinvestment of both dividends and capital gains in additional shares, liquidity and share exchange privileges.

Net Asset Value (NAV) - This is the value of a mutual fund's assets, minus its liabilities, which is divided by the total number of shares outstanding. The Net Asset Value is published daily in most newspapers.

No-Load Mutual Fund - A mutual fund that does not charge a commission to buy shares in the fund. About half of all mutual funds are No-Load-Funds.

Sector Mutual Funds - Mutual funds that invest in specific sectors of the economy, such as computers, utilities or biotechnology. They may also invest in specific countries or regions of the world. There are a vast array of very specific Sector Mutual Funds than one can choose to invest through.

CHAPTER
◆ 9 ◆

RESIDENTIAL REAL ESTATE

Medium to Long Yardage Gainer

Approximately 67% of the U.S. population lives in owner-occupied residential property. Home ownership has its obvious attractions, but the factors you need to consider rationally before buying a home are somewhat less apparent. This chapter will assist you with respect to three of the most important areas regarding a home purchase. Answering these questions can help smooth some of the bumps out of what can sometimes be a challenging process:

- Why should you consider buying a home.
- When and where should you buy a home.
- How to finance your purchase and minimize closing costs.

WHY BUY A HOME?

EMOTIONAL REWARDS

There are both emotional and financial reasons why you should consider buying a home. People usually find more satisfaction in living in their own home, than they do in renting. Most homeowners enjoy a greater degree of privacy. They can make changes to their property without consulting a landlord. Home ownership also tends to enhance our sense of personal security. Even in today's highly mobile society, most of us have a greater sense of belonging to a community when we live in a home we own.

FINANCIAL REWARDS

The financial rewards can be just as satisfying as the emotional ones. As a rule, purchasing a home is a sound financial investment. Residential property ordinarily appreciates in value over any ten to twenty year period. Since World War II, the appreciation rate has exceeded the inflation rate. Millions of people are now living in financial circumstances beyond what they ever imagined in their teens or twenties, mainly because the residential property they purchased has appreciated so much in value over the long term.

On the other hand, home values have plummeted regionally for periods of time. The Southern California housing market of the early 1990s stands out as the most recent example of a regional real estate slump. There are some relatively easy strategies you can use to minimize the possibility of being caught in one of these downward depreciation spirals after purchasing your new home.

Usually the monthly mortgage payment remains the same amount each month. Some homeowners, however, have a variable rate mortgage wherein the monthly payment can increase or decrease depending on some financial index. The monthly rate remains constant if the buyer has a fixed rate mortgage. With a fixed rate mortgage, the interest charged on the mortgage loan is the same for the duration of the mortgage or the first major portion of the mortgage. If your mortgage payment includes the property taxes, hazard insurance, or private mortgage insurance (PMI), your monthly payment will increase with an increase in any of these items. Incidentally, when these items are paid with the mortgage, it is called an impound account. In other words, the account impounds PITI—principal, interest, taxes and insurance.

TAX INCENTIVES

The government offers tax incentives to encourage people to own their own home. You can deduct mortgage interest payments from your income tax. To get this deduction, simply fill out Schedule A of Federal Income Tax Form 1040.

In 1986, Congress enacted some mortgage interest deduction restrictions. These restrictions have only affected a small percentage of taxpayers who have high mortgage loans. Regardless of any significant tax code changes that may occur in the future, such as the so-called flat tax that periodically receives media attention, the home mortgage interest deduction is likely to remain unchanged. It is too popular a deduction for either the Republican or Democratic parties to consider changing.

In addition to deducting mortgage interest from your taxes, you can also defer any capital gains realized from the sale of a residential home indefinitely. In order to do this, simply purchase and occupy another home of equal or greater cost than your current home within twenty-four months of the date you closed its sale.

Not only can the capital gains earned on the sale of a home be tax deferred, but much if not all of this gain can be exempt from taxation for those age 55 or older, provided some conditions are met. This is known as a homeowner's once-in-a-lifetime capital gains income tax exclusion. The profit does not have to be obtained on the same home to be exempt. It could be the result of profits gained from having lived in several homes. The person must have owned and lived in the last home, as his or her principal residence, for at least three of the previous five years. Anyone who might be eligible for this capital gains tax exclusion should consult both his or her accountant and the current tax code.

WHEN SHOULD YOU PURCHASE A HOME?

In the 1970s and 1980s, it was relatively easy to answer the question of when to buy a home. During this period, there was almost no bad time to buy in most of the country. Prices appreciated dramatically during the latter half of both decades and remained relatively stable for the other half.

It is probably true to say that residential real estate prices have not appreciated in value as much in any two consecutive decades as it did during the 1970s and 1980s. We are unlikely to see such an escalation in prices in such a short period for decades to come. Nevertheless, a home purchase can still be a solid financial investment and personally rewarding. You can dramatically increase your chances of making a wise home purchase by spending some time following and understanding the basics of the economic news.

IS THE ECONOMY EXPANDING OR CONTRACTING?

In decades past, many people who purchased homes had little awareness or interest in the economic news. Since the economic recovery from the Great Depression of the 1930s, most economic downturns have been relatively short-lived. Brief recessions and generally good corporate prospects led workers to believe in unending job security, particularly in the decades following the second world war.

The comparatively long recession of the early 1990s marked a departure from the overall trend of uninterrupted prosperity. The period ushered in a harsh new reality of corporate down-sizing and employee expendability. For the first time in recent memory, economic conditions shook workers from their sense of security.

Because the general economy affects the housing sector, it is imperative that you pay very close attention to the economic news, especially if you are a first-time home buyer. You should know how strong or weak the economy is and whether it is expanding or contracting, not only in the country as a whole, but also in your own region. Chapter 13 of this book, "Understanding the Economic News," will provide you with the tools you need to grasp information presented in the economic news. You should also consult several of the many superb, easy-to-read books that can guide you in understanding the basics about our economy. Once you've mastered those fundamentals, you will find a wealth of important economic and financial news in your local newspaper, certain business and finance magazines and specific television programs.

SO WHEN SHOULD YOU BUY A HOME?

As a general rule, first-time home buyers should purchase a home as the economy is coming out of a recession. Usually, the economy is well out of a downturn and even booming when some first-time home buyers start shopping for a home. This delay causes many to buy at the height of an economic expansion or when there are some signs of an economic slowdown. Because they lack the basic knowledge of how to interpret the major economic indicators, they have missed an opportunity to benefit from an upturn in home prices. This missed opportunity can be financially crucial for the first-time buyer—and even the experienced home buyer.

ASSESS YOUR PERSONAL CIRCUMSTANCES

Once you have a clear understanding of where the regional and national economy is at in its expansion and contraction cycle, you need to assess your own particular circumstances.

Many factors may influence your decision to purchase a home, such as a need for more space because of a growing family, a job transfer or a preference to live in a particular area. You should also closely evaluate your job security. It can be financially devastating and emotionally demoralizing to buy a home and then find yourself laid off work because of down-sizing or a change in the economy, your company or industry.

Of course, no one has a crystal ball that allows them to see clearly into the economic future—not even the President or the Federal Reserve Board chairman. So try to make your decision prudently, always realizing that you cannot control every variable. You can, however, discreetly research the performance of your company and industry.

Watch for possible downturn indicators within your company. Such clues as hiring freezes, overtime cuts, expense cuts and other "belt tightening" measures, supply shortages or inventory declines, and a drop-off in customer demand could foretell problems ahead. Also check the financial press for economic "health reports" about your company and your industry. Your home-buying decision should take into account your family's potential future needs, financial circumstances and also the projected state of the economy over a three-to four-year period.

WHERE TO BUY A HOME

For many, the decision of where to buy is relatively easy, but deciding which home you should buy in your preferred area is another story altogether. Many buyers are not sure what kind of home they want. This can be an emotionally challenging ordeal for many house hunters and their families. There are just so many people to please and emotions to soothe. Add to this the fear many people often have making decisions involving high financial commitments, even when they know they have found the right house, in the right area, at a good price and at a good time in the economic cycle, and then you'll really have a stew of emotions stirring!

At best, you'll need to do a lot of homework and leg work to buy intelligently. But house hunting can be particularly trying if you are unfamiliar with the area in which you are considering buying.

BUYING IN AN UNFAMILIAR AREA

First, drive around the general area several times, preferably on your own, in order to avoid any distractions. This can be a particularly positive strategy for many couples and families. You'll probably want to find out if the community's services and your potential neighbors foster the kind of lifestyle you are seeking. Visit supermarkets, stores and various gathering places in order to get a sense of the kind of people who live in the area.

Take a weekday to visit the Chamber of Commerce and obtain their brochures about the town and area. Use the resources of any visitors' center or "welcome wagon" the community may have. Purchase the local newspaper and read about the area. Visit the city or town hall and pick up brochures about programs and services. Learn about public parks and recreation centers, community courses and recreational facilities.

Residents of the community you're looking into can provide you with valuable information. Try to talk to some people who live in the area, either at a coffee shop or some other establishments where it's easy to meet people. Drop in on the neighborhood public library's weekly discussion group—or any neighborhood activity that interest you—to meet and talk with your prospective neighbors. Ask active PTA officers about their impressions of the local school.

There is perhaps no better way to find out if your prospective neighbors and the city actively support and foster desirable qualities in a community than through its neighborhood action groups. These groups can help you gauge the community's commitment to remedying any potential problems, such as traffic congestion, pedestrian safety or personal security. Peruse bulletin boards in libraries and other public locales for announcements of neighborhood meetings and issues that concern your prospective neighborhood. Attend a meeting, if you can find the time. If you can't find time, you could look at a meeting agenda and talk to people on the phone. Do this several times. It can take a while to get a true sense of an area that you are not familiar with.

Your Chamber of Commerce can provide you with some useful data; however, keep in mind that their information is skewed to promote goodwill towards area businesses. Although realtors can provide valuable information about schools, churches, entertainment, sports, recreational activities, crime and other matters, you should avoid them during these initial stages so that you do not feel pressured into making a decision prematurely. You need to form your own impressions because you will be the one living in the house you buy—not the boosters and real estate people.

The community police station and the public library can provide objective data about crime and security in an area. It might be helpful to talk with the neighborhood block captain, someone who interacts with the local police and the rest of the community to report or mitigate security problems.

You can even check the city planning commission's reports and look into planned highway and commercial construction (you don't want to move in and then find a freeway or airport addition going up in your backyard). You can find out some of this information from a glance at a publicly posted city council meeting agenda.

Save time by checking the Internet. More and more cities and visitor's bureaus, even in modest-sized communities, are "wired" to the Internet with web pages that inform residents about issues, entertainment and recreational opportunities. Although you'll feel exhausted from all this legwork, you will then be in a much better position to make an intelligent home-buying decision.

FINANCING YOUR HOME PURCHASE

Rarely does a home buyer have the cash on hand to purchase a home outright. Some form of financing must be arranged. Banks, savings and loans, mortgage companies and private parties finance most home purchases. Historically, the pattern has been for a buyer to put down 20% of the purchase price and for a lender to finance the remaining 80% for 30 years, with either a fixed or a variable interest rate. Today, many buyers are obtaining loans for almost the whole purchase price. Currently, there are more options for home loan financing than even 20 years ago.

The first area of concern for many home buyers, especially first-time home buyers, is how much of the purchase price they can get financed. Often, they would like all of it to be financed because they do not have cash readily available for a down payment. There are 100% financing programs available. The best way to find out about them is through your major local Sunday newspaper, which usually devotes a large section to real estate news and sales.

HOW MUCH SHOULD YOU FINANCE?

If mortgage interest rates are at historically low levels, as they were during part of the 1990s, then consider financing as much as you can of the mortgage. This can be a very intelligent strategy even for a person who would have no problem putting 20% to 40% down. The money they might have used for a down payment can instead be invested for greater stock market returns. Remember that all mortgage interest paid is an itemized tax deduction—unless the mortgage loan is more than a million dollars for joint tax filers.

QUALIFYING FOR A LOAN

The typical buyer goes house hunting first and shops for a loan later. You should reverse this process. Although the first major concern of most home buyers is how much of the purchase price they can finance, they should establish initially how much of a loan they can qualify for. The process of determining in advance how much money you can borrow is called "mortgage loan pre-qualification." Although time-consuming, it can eliminate a lot of frustration later.

Using the real estate section of your newspaper as a reference, make a list of the major local mortgage companies, their interest rates and contact information, including phone numbers. Call several and ask for information on their various mortgage loan programs. After you have narrowed your list, call and ask them how much of a loan you can pre-qualify for. It will take some homework on your part to make sense of the various options, especially if you feel like a novice in this area of personal finance. Do not pay for pre-qualification or make any loan commitment at this time.

FIXED OR VARIABLE INTEREST RATE?

Next, you need to decide whether to go with a fixed or variable interest rate loan. Usually a person can qualify for a bigger mortgage by selecting a variable rate loan. But you should not to do this just to qualify for a higher loan amount. If fixed interest rates are at historically low levels, then you should obtain a fixed rate loan for the duration of your mortgage.

Remember, a fixed interest rate gives you the security of knowing how much your monthly payment is going to be every month for the life of your mortgage. When mortgage interest rates are higher than 8%, many buyers choose a variable rate mortgage.

Mortgage lenders offer many types of variable interest rate programs.

You should definitely have pen and paper handy in order to do some basic math calculations. You can, for example, obtain a variable rate mortgage—sometimes called an adjustable rate mortgage—that can change once every year for the duration of the loan, but never exceeds a certain percentage rate, such as 12%.

Your contract will state when the interest rate changes. The change in rate, whether up or down, is tied to a particular financial index that is independent of the mortgage company. Examples of such financial indexes are the one-year U.S. Treasury bill rate, three-month certificate of deposit (CD) and the prime rate.

Again, your Sunday newspaper's real estate section lists most of these indexes. These indexes do not move exactly in the same direction or at the same time. Therefore, it can be very difficult to decide which index to choose if you are unfamiliar with how they respond to various economic conditions.

Some mortgage lenders offer variable or adjustable rate mortgages with a payment cap but no interest rate cap. You should avoid these. Even though the monthly payment is capped, the interest rate could go through the roof. Paying off such a loan could take forever because the lender can add on the extra interest at the end of the scheduled payments.

POINTS

You should familiarize yourself with the concept of points (reviewed again in the closing costs section). Points are another relatively new wrinkle (within the last 30 years) in mortgage financing. When you hear the word point or points, just think prepaid interest made to the lender. One point is equal to 1% of the loan. So one point on a $100,000 mortgage is $1,000. The more points you pay at escrow closing, the lower your interest rate will be.

SHOULD YOU PAY POINTS?

How do you decide whether or not to prepay points in order to have a lower interest rate? It depends on many factors. For example, if interest rates are at historically low levels—as they were during parts of the 1990s—and you plan to stay in the home for more than seven years, then you should, if you can, pay at least one or two points in order to reduce your interest rate. A lower interest rate would result in lower payments. If you prepay points with a separate check, the costs are usually tax deductible on a home purchase on your income tax form. The tax rules are different on paying points when refinancing a home loan.

You should obtain a mortgage amortization booklet at your local bookstore in order to mathematically calculate the payments with different interest rates. If, for example, mortgage interest rates are at relatively high historical levels and you foresee a likely reduction in the years ahead, then you probably should not prepay any points.

If, as you project, interest rates do come down, then it will likely be advantageous to refinance and get a new loan. That's when you should consider paying points in order to get a lower rate. Remember that it takes several years to recoup in lower payments the amount of prepaid points. The longer you are paying on the same mortgage, the more beneficial it is to prepay points. The shorter you are paying on the same mortgage, the less beneficial it is to prepay points. This is a general guideline to help you decide wisely.

CLOSING COSTS

Let's now turn to an area of home buying that even leaves veterans of the game in a daze. It's called closing costs. By tradition, a neutral third party handles the paperwork and monies relative to a home purchase. This third party process is called escrow. It may be known by another name in your part of the country. Even before escrow opens, you should become familiar with most of the items that appear on the escrow closing statement. To the uninitiated, many of the items or entries that appear on an escrow closing statement may seem at first to be written in a language other than English! A fundamental understanding of closing statement entries will help you enormously, thus making your home purchase experience easier and more satisfying. It will certainly help to keep your nerves from fraying!

BUYER'S CLOSING COSTS OR SETTLEMENT STATEMENT

There are two closing statements—one for the seller and one for the buyer. We are going to review the buyer's closing statement. Your statement may contain most of the following items:

Points (Discount Points or Loan Discount Fee)
Loan Origination Fee
Broker's Commission
Title Insurance
Lender's Document Preparation Fee
Private Mortgage Insurance (PMI)
Appraisal Fee
Homeowner's Insurance (Fire or Hazard Insurance)
Escrow Fee
Credit Report Fee
Transfer or Assumption Fee or Tax
Lender's Inspection Fee
Private Mortgage Insurance Application Fee
Notary Fee
Termite and Other Inspection Fee
Mortgage insurance
Other Miscellaneous Fees

POINTS

Points, as already briefly reviewed, are a cost that a lender may add to the basic mortgage charge. Each point represents 1% of the face value of the loan. So if there is one point charged on a $100,000 loan, the cost for the point is $1,000. Points are negotiable. If you do not want to pay any points, then the lender will charge a higher interest rate. No one can advise you correctly whether to pay points or accept a higher interest rate without knowing some variables, such as how long you are planning to keep the home, current market interest rates, the state of the economy—both nationally and locally—and how much cash on hand you have to make a down payment and also pay for closing costs. The IRS usually regards any loan points costs as prepaid interest and will allow you to itemize this charge on Schedule A of the Federal Income Tax form. A knowledge of some basic mathematics and a real estate loan amortization booklet can really help in making an intelligent decision about your mortgage loan.

LOAN ORIGINATION FEE

The lender charges this fee for the administrative costs of processing the loan and it is often expressed as a percentage of the loan. The buyer usually pays the loan origination fee. Whether the buyer pays a loan origination fee or the lender charges one is a negotiable item. It may be negotiated so that the seller pays the origination fee. Since it is one of the main closing cost expenses, you should be willing to negotiate the cost of this item.

BROKER'S COMMISSION

This is the commission paid to the real estate brokerage office that listed the property for sale and also to the office that sold the property. Commissions for the sale of a personal residence are normally an expense item to the seller. It is usually the largest expense item to appear on the sellers closing statement. Real estate sales commissions are negotiable. They are not set by law but by the custom in the area.

TITLE INSURANCE

Most home buyers have no idea what title insurance is. It is important that you always have a good title insurance policy, even if you pay cash for a home. Title insurance guarantees that you will be paid up to the limits in the insurance policy if you lose title to the property because of a prior hidden claim. Title insurance is a one time charge. Title insurance policies are issued and sold by title insurance companies. You may be able to assume the existing title insurance policy on the property and incur a lesser charge than by purchasing a brand new policy. Although it is standard procedure for the buyer to pay for his or her own title insurance, it is a negotiable item. Sometimes the seller will offer to pay for it in order to close the sale. Your realtor should make sure that you have a policy with a financially strong title company. A.M. Best rates the financial strength of title insurance companies in the same way as it rates fire and casualty and life insurance companies.

LENDER'S DOCUMENT PREPARATION FEE
This fee may be included in the loan origination fee or itemized as an additional fee. As the name suggests, the document preparation fee covers the preparation of final legal papers, such as a mortgage deed of trust, note or deed. This fee is also negotiable with the lender. It depends on how much the lender wants the loan, how much you want the loan, your bargaining skills and also whether it is a sellers or buyers market.

PRIVATE MORTGAGE INSURANCE (PMI)
Any loan that is greater than 80% of the Loan-to-Value (LTV) and made by anyone other than a private party usually requires private mortgage insurance (PMI). Private mortgage insurance (PMI) guarantees that the lender will be paid by the insurance company in the event the buyer defaults on the loan. It is both an up front and recurring cost for the buyer. Many lenders do not require the buyer to continue paying for PMI when the loan is 80% or less of the property's value. The buyer can request in writing that PMI be omitted. After the lender verifies through an appraisal that the loan is 80% or less of the property's market value, the lender generally deletes the PMI charge.

One way that many buyers avoid PMI, even though they have borrowed over 80% of the purchase price, is to require the seller to carry back a second mortgage of 10%, or more of the sales price. Many buyers have obtained even better financing—at a lower interest rate—from the seller than they could have from a mortgage or bank lender. This often happens when the real estate market is a "buyers market." In this market, sellers greatly outnumber buyers. This phenomenon occurred in many parts of the country during the first half of the 1990s.

APPRAISAL FEE

Either an independent appraiser or the lender charges an appraisal fee for determining the current market value of the home being purchased. This fee varies, depending on the lender, the appraiser, the property and the real estate market. This is a one-time cost and a negotiable item and can be paid by the buyer or seller.

FIRE INSURANCE

A mortgage lender requires at least a fire policy with "special form coverage." But you should have more coverage than this. Consult your insurance agent or broker about adequate coverage. Lenders require that it be issued by a financially strong insurance company and so should you. The cost is both an up front and recurring charge. The price will vary by company, the area and the amount of coverage. If your property is located in a federally identified flood zone, the lender will likely require flood insurance as well as fire insurance. Mortgage companies do not usually require earthquake insurance, even in shaky California.

ESCROW FEE

The escrow office assesses this fee for keeping track of all the appropriate papers and data from various sources. The escrow agent must comply strictly with the original purchase and sales agreement. They are called escrow instructions.

CREDIT REPORT FEE

This fee covers the cost of a credit report. Sometimes the lender uses an outside agency to get these detailed reports. You may be able to get this charge waived if you supply a current copy of your credit record from Experian (formerly TRW), Transunion and Equifax. A good credit record is very important in qualifying for the best prevailing interest rate.

TRANSFER OR ASSUMPTION FEE

When a buyer takes over—assumes—an existing mortgage or loan on a property, a transfer or assumption fee is assessed. Like many other charges, this fee can be negotiated.

LENDER'S INSPECTION FEE

Either the lending institution or a private inspection company carries out and charges a fee for an inspection, which is usually done on newly constructed homes.

PRIVATE MORTGAGE INSURANCE APPLICATION FEE

This is a one-time negotiable fee for processing an application for private mortgage insurance (PMI).

NOTARY FEE

To guarantee signatures on certain legal documents, the buyer must pay this nominal one-time fee to a notary. The notary is usually an escrow officer.

TERMITE AND OTHER PEST INSPECTIONS

Lenders vary in their inspection requirements. Either the buyer or the seller pays the fee for any required inspections.

OTHER MISCELLANEOUS FEES

There are likely to be at least a few items on your closing statement that make absolutely no sense, regardless of how they are explained. What, for instance, is a warehouse or title company sub-escrow fee? These fees sometimes appear on escrow closing statements. Just make sure you have a clear understanding of the major charges. If you try to understand and make sense out of each and every charge, you will leave little time for what should be a pleasant and exciting experience. Don't try to know it all, unless of course, you are like a sponge with data.

SUMMARY

If you have read this chapter in one sitting you may feel you need a mini-cruise to clear your head! The amount of information is greater and more detailed than on the other investment players—stocks, bonds, money market securities, savings accounts and mutual funds. But if you focus initially on just knowing the central points and build from there, you will find this chapter very valuable.

These are the important areas to be aware of right now:

- There are emotional and financial advantages to buying a home.
- The economy's expansion and contraction cycles have a powerful impact on the market value of homes. Home prices generally increase as the economy grows and they decrease when it is in a recession. If you know what is happening with the major economic indicators (discussed later in Chapter 13, "Understanding The Economic News") you will easily be able to follow whether the economy is growing, strong, contracting or in a recession.
- Be prepared to spend quite some time and energy in the process of finding a home you will be happy with. This is especially true if you have a spouse and children to consider and also if you are not very familiar with the area you want to buy a home.
- Your personal and financial circumstances play a key role in the kind of home you should purchase. Your job stability and credit rating or credit record are two of the most important factors to keep in mind when you are house hunting.
- There are currently many loan financing options available. For example, do you go with a fixed or variable rate mortgage? Should you pay points or not?
- Closing costs are a major expense in buying or selling a home.

YOUR RESIDENTIAL REAL ESTATE INVESTING GAME PLAN

🏈 *Become familiar with Chapter 13 titled—"Understanding the Economic News,"—especially if you have never purchased—or sold—a home before.* Gain a basic knowledge about the economy so you'll be able to recognize upturn and downturn cycles. As we've observed, the onset of an economic recovery foretells an impending increase in property values. Conversely, when the economy is in a deep recession, you can expect housing values to decline.

🏈 *If you are considering buying in an area that you are not very familiar with, be prepared to do considerable legwork and driving.* Drive around the area, preferably on your own. Make inquiries as you go along. Read the local newspaper. Visit the chamber of commerce and city hall. They can provide a wealth of information.

🏈 *Learn about the basic financing options available.* The sheer amount of adjustable or variable rate mortgages and fixed rate mortgages can be staggering, particularly for a beginner. Be patient as you try to sift through them in your effort to make an intelligent choice.

🏈 *Become familiar with the major expense charges that appear on an escrow closing statement.* Many experienced home buyers have some difficulty understanding the varied charges. It does initially look intimidating, so break it down and study what each is for.

🏈 *Organize your notes and documents.* Set up several manila folders for each of the major areas. Most of the documents pertaining to a home purchase are done on legal size paper, so they can be cumbersome to organize and read. We are much more used to handling $8^1/_2$ x 11 inch or letter size paper. Set up a folder for at least each of the following areas: closing

150

costs, financing, data on the location, taxes, insurance, applications and credit record.

◆ *Get acquainted with the terminology at the end of this chapter.* It is extensive, so take your time!

◆ *Read books for the first-time home buyer.* For a more thorough reading on the home buying and financing process read: *100 Questions Every First Time Home Buyer Should Ask* by Ilyce Glink and also *The 106 Common Mistakes Homebuyers Make* by Dr. Gary Eldred.

You'll find information about mail ordering these and other books at the conclusion of this book.

RESIDENTIAL REAL ESTATE— TERMINOLOGY

Abstract of Title - It summarizes the past ownership of a property and includes any changes in ownership, mortgages, liens, charges and any other historical information about the title.

Acceleration Clause - This clause in a mortgage agreement states that if the borrower defaults on the payment schedule, the remaining payments may become immediately due and payable at once, at the request of the lender.

Adjustable Rate Mortgage (ARM) - Also known as a variable rate mortgage. With an ARM, the interest rate is set at the beginning of the mortgage but it can vary at certain times thereafter. The future interest rate charged depends on market conditions. Adjustable Rate Mortgages usually have a top interest rate cap stated in the mortgage contract. When interest rates are relatively high, many borrowers opt for an ARM. When interest rates are at relatively low levels, say under 8%, most borrowers choose a thirty-year fixed interest rate mortgage.

Amortized Loan - A loan that is paid off in equal payments over a specified period of time, usually thirty years. If you are considering purchasing a home in the foreseeable future, buy a mortgage amortization booklet. It is available for a nominal cost at your local bookstore.

Appraisal Fee - Professional appraisers charge a fee to estimate the market value of a home at the time of purchase. The cost of an appraisal is a negotiable item with respect to who pays for it.

Assumption of Mortgage - The ability of a buyer to take over responsibility for paying an existing mortgage. This does not release the seller of his or her mortgage obligation, unless consented to by the lender.

Balloon Payment - Much larger than the other payments. This is the final payment on a certain type of loan.

Binder - In real estate, this term refers to the initial contract form that specifies the main preliminary items of agreement which will be replaced later with a more formal and detailed contract.

Buyer's Market - This expression describes a real estate market in which sellers significantly outnumber buyers. Consequently the buyers can dictate more favorable terms than in a sellers market, where there are many buyers but few sellers. Generally, during an economic recession it is a buyers market and during boom economic times it is a sellers market.

Closing Costs - These are the fees paid at the close of escrow. Many Closing Costs are negotiable. Some Closing Costs can sound very unfamiliar to first-time and even second-time home buyers. The list of Closing Costs, never mind the names given to some of them, can make a person's head spin. If you have never purchased a home but are planning to do so in the near future, become familiar with at least the major Closing Costs.

Closing Statement - A statement at the end of escrow where all the provisions of the purchase and sale have been documented. It summarizes the various items and their charges for both the buyer and seller. Many first-time buyers scratch their heads in bewilderment at the number of items that appear on a Closing Statement; never mind what they *all* mean.

Conforming Loan - This is a mortgage loan that conforms to guidelines of Freddie Mac (FHLMC) and Fannie Mae (FNMA), two national mortgage buyers. Virtually all mortgage loans made today conform to their guidelines.

Contingency Offer - An offer to purchase a home but with a certain Contingency Offer, or perhaps several contingencies attached. For example, a buyer may purchase a home on the contingency that their own home sells first or that the seller makes certain repairs.

Conventional Mortgage - A mortgage made with a 20 % down payment, with the balance financed by a thirty-year fixed rate mortgage. This was the typical mortgage about thirty years ago. Today, there is a vast array of options for financing a home purchase. Under certain circumstances, many lenders will now finance 100 % of the purchase price, including closing costs. Having a good credit rating is one of the most important factors.

Credit Report - A report that records the credit history of a mortgage borrower. It plays a critical role in determining the best interest rate a borrower can obtain. Every home buyer should have a copy of his or her Credit Record from at least one of the three major credit data companies—Experian (formerly TRW), Transunion and Equifax—before purchasing a home.

Default - A failure to make payments as agreed on in a mortgage contract. The lender usually begins foreclosure proceedings after the borrower fails to make several payments.

Depreciation - The decrease in value of a property due to age and wear and tear. Although rental property may depreciate physically and thus generate a tax deduction, it usually increases in market value at the same time.

Down Payment - The amount of his or her own money that a buyer pays to purchase a home. Some buyers put nothing down. They finance or get a mortgage loan for the full purchase price. It is much easier for buyers with a good credit record to purchase a home without making a Down Payment than it is for those buyers with a marginal or poor credit history.

Due-On-Sale Clause - This Clause allows a lender to legally require the mortgage to be paid in full in the event that the home is sold. A Due-On-Sale Clause is in the mortgage contract in order to prevent a buyer from assuming the existing loan without the lender's consent.

Equity Build Up - The increase in a persons ownership of a home resulting from a decrease in the mortgage loan balance and any increase in the market value of the property.

Escrow - The neutral third party that handles all the paperwork between the seller and buyer. The escrow closing period can vary in length from sale to sale. The buyer or seller can stipulate in the purchase contract how long or short escrow can be. A payment or penalty is paid by the party that does not abide by this time period, if indeed there is a time period stated in the purchase or sales contract.

Falling-Out-Of-Escrow - A real estate term in which one of the parties to the real estate contract does not fulfill their obligations and so the deal falls apart or Falls-Out-Of-Escrow. There can be financial consequences or penalties for failing to complete all of the escrow or contract requirements.

Federal Housing Administration (FHA) - An agency within the U.S. Department of Housing and Urban Development (HUD) that provides financial support for certain homebuyers.

First Mortgage - Or senior mortgage. Some buyers may get an 80% loan-to-value (LTV) and then have the seller finance 10% or more of the purchase price. In this situation, the sellers loan will be in second position to the 80% loan. If the buyer defaults paying the second loan, the first mortgagee is entitled to be paid from the proceeds of the sale of the home, if it is foreclosed.

Fixed Rate Mortgage - Usually refers to a mortgage with an interest rate that remains the same for the life of the loan. Some mortgage loans have a Fixed Rate for ten years or some other time interval and then it varies with market conditions.

Foreclosure - A legal process whereby the lender takes back all rights to the property, including the right of the borrower to live in the property. It is generally caused by the failure of the borrower to make the payments as agreed to in the loan contract. Sometimes a property is foreclosed because the property taxes on it have not been paid.

Home Inspection Service - An inspection that a buyer may require before escrow closes. This inspection is done in order to find any defects or problems with the home. All homebuyers should have a home inspection performed by a licensed and competent inspector.

Index - Adjustable rate mortgages (ARMs) change their interest rates based on the movement of certain indexes, such as the one-year U.S. Treasury bill, or the prime rate. The Index used is specified in the mortgage agreement. It is very difficult, even for experienced homebuyers, to determine which is the most favorable Index to use if they are deciding to use an adjustable rate mortgage (ARM). Although all of these mortgage indexes respond somewhat the same to market conditions, they can have significant variations from time-to-time.

Interest Rate Cap - This term refers to the top interest rate that can be charged as specified in the mortgage agreement in an adjustable rate mortgage. For example, an adjustable rate mortgage (ARM) may start out at 3.75% and have a maximum Interest Rate Cap of 11%.

Joint Tenancy - Most homeowners have the title to their property held in Joint Tenancy. Commonly, a husband and wife will hold title in Joint Tenancy. If one spouse dies, the survivor automatically owns the property without probate or a will. This is one of several ways a person can hold title to a home.

Jumbo Loans - In the language of real estate financing, there are basically two types of loans—conforming loans and Jumbo Loans—that stipulate the amount that a mortgage loan must be under, in order to be a conforming loan. Fannie Mae and Freddie Mac set the guidelines. Any mortgage over this amount is called a Jumbo Loan. The interest rate charged for a Jumbo Loan is slightly higher than a conforming loan, if all other factors are the same.

Lease Option Contract - A method of purchasing a home wherein a buyer rents a property for a specified period of time, say two years, and then agrees to purchase the home at that time for a stated price in the Lease Option Contract. If the prospective buyer does not buy the property, he or she forfeits the Lease Option deposit, which was set by the seller. Usually a certain amount of the rent goes towards the down payment in a Lease Option Contract. Lease Option Contracts can have many negotiated variables. It can be a great method for some people to purchase or sell a home.

Listing - A contract between a real estate broker and a seller, giving the broker the right to sell the home at a specific price.

Loan Commitment - An agreement made by a mortgage company or other entity to finance a home purchase for a certain amount and a stated interest rate before the final documents have been signed. This is an important commitment for a buyer to have before spending more time and money on purchasing a home. It can eliminate any surprises and aggravation later in the home buying process.

Loan Origination Fee - This is a fee charged by mortgage lenders for the paperwork processing. Typically, it is 1 % of the loan amount. It is a negotiable item. Many buyers are not aware of this fee until they have committed a lot of time and money to the home buying process. It appears as one of the costs in the escrow closing statement.

Loan-To-Value (LTV) - The amount of the loan expressed as a percentage of the total purchase price. If the purchase price is higher than what the lender appraises the property to be worth, the buyer may have a serious financial problem. A home that sells and appraises for $200,000, which has a loan commitment of $160,000, is said to have an 80 % Loan-To-Value (LTV) ratio.

Mortgage Broker - A person or company that obtains mortgages for others. Instead of working with one lender, a Mortgage Broker shops many lenders for the best rates and terms. At least that is the idea in theory. Often, it does not pan out that way. Many mortgage brokers have gouged their unsuspecting and uninformed home buyers. Having a basic knowledge of the mortgage financing process will protect you from unscrupulous brokers. Do not rely just on the recommendation of friends, coworkers or an attorney.

Mortgage Interest Deduction - Although many forms of interest were eliminated as an income tax deduction in the so-called Tax Reform Act of 1986, the home Mortgage Interest Deduction remained virtually as it was before. Mortgage interest is deductible from Federal Income Tax , up to a specified amount on a persons principal home. If the owners are filing jointly, the mortgage loan cannot exceed $1 Million dollars in order for all the interest paid to be income tax deductible.

Points - Also known as discount points. You may hear points explained in many ways, particularly by a mortgage lender. Points are simply prepaid interest. One point means 1% of the loan. For example, a $200,000 loan with a one point charge means 1% of $200,000, which is $2,000. A person can obtain a zero point loan but the interest charged on the loan is higher.

Prepayment Penalty - Sometimes a mortgage company will charge a penalty if a mortgage is prepaid before the scheduled date. The mortgage contract will specify if there is a prepayment penalty or not.

Principal - Initially, this refers to the actual amount borrowed. As payments are made, the Principal is the balance of the mortgage, less interest charges.

Property Taxes - Taxes levied on property that are used to pay for schools and other government projects. These taxes are levied by states, cities and other government agencies. Property Taxes can be itemized as a deduction on Federal Income Tax Form 1040.

Refinancing - Paying off an existing mortgage and negotiating a new one. Usually homeowners refinance when interest rates decline. Refinancing is not free. Therefore, do some calculations first before signing on the dotted line. A basic knowledge about the economy and Federal Reserve Board interest rate changes can be a great help in making an intelligent decision in this area.

Seller Financing - Home financing that is offered by the seller. Usually this is in the form of a second mortgage. In the event of foreclosure, the first mortgage is paid off before the second. Many buyers do not investigate the possibility of Seller Financing. If the sellers are getting a price that they are happy with, they may be willing to finance all or a portion of the purchase price at more favorable rates and conditions than are generally available on the open market.

Teaser Rate - This is a below market rate that is often advertised by lenders on adjustable rate mortgages (ARMs). This rate is usually adjusted upwards after the deal has closed. It is important for buyers to examine an adjustable rate contract. A basic familiarity with these contracts, long before considering a home purchase can be of enormous help when the time comes to go house hunting. There are many pieces that need to be pulled together, often on short notice and when emotions are likely to be high. This is why a little preplanning can pay off handsomely later.

Title Insurance - Good Title Insurance is something every homebuyer should have, even if they pay cash and do not finance any of the purchase. It guarantees title to the property in the event any doubt is raised about legal ownership of the home. The insurance company will pay the stated amount in the insurance policy to the title policy owner. Just as mortgage companies will not finance a loan without a fire policy, neither will they finance a home loan without a Title Insurance policy from a financially strong insurance company.

Transfer Fee - A closing cost for officially transferring title to the property from the seller to the buyer.

PART IV

Tax Advantaged Investing

◆

Supercharge Your Offense

CHAPTER

◆ 10 ◆

TAX SHELTERED INVESTMENT PLANS

401K, 403B, Sep-Ira, Ira, Keogh Plan, Real Estate, Roth Ira and Others

SUPERCHARGE YOUR OFFENSE

Many investments can be supercharged through the intelligent use of our tax laws. Both the federal and state governments have enacted many tax laws that encourage particular types of investing. By using these tax laws wisely, you can increase your chances of becoming a great quarterback of your investment plan. Think of these tax laws as great offensive protectors and guards that help your investment players to reach your goal line faster than you would otherwise. Many tax strategies that people utilize are exclusively defensive in nature. They only help to reduce a person's tax liability. Others are such that they not only help to reduce current taxes but also speed along the attainment of our investment and financial goals. In this and the next two chapters, we'll focus on some of the most frequently used tax sheltered investment plans.

401 K

A 401K is a qualified salary reducing plan that is offered by many employers. Typically, it is offered by companies with over one hundred employees. The paperwork and costs of setting up a 401K and continuing to administer it are extensive. Consequently, many employers do not see any positive value in it for them. Nevertheless, the number of employers setting up 401Ks and the number of employees contributing to them in the past twenty years has skyrocketed. With a 401K, a certain amount of an employee's salary is withheld and invested inside the plan. The monies withheld and invested inside a 401K are not subject to current income taxation. Congress sets the amount of currently tax exempt salary that an employee can have withheld. This figure usually increases every year.

HOW ARE THE MONIES INSIDE A 401K INVESTED?

Until several years ago, the choices were limited. At the moment, the selections available are overwhelming for many of today's employees. The amount of basic investment education has not kept pace with the increase in the number of options that are usually available with most 401K plans. In the past, about all that was available was a stock fund, a bond fund and a money market fund. Today, one can likely select from a broad range of more specific funds. A review of the chapter on mutual funds will help you understand the major categories of mutual funds. Later, as you delve deeper into this area, you will see how people can narrow the focus of their investments.

EMPLOYER CONTRIBUTIONS TO 401KS

Many employers will match a portion of the employee's contribution to his or her 401K. Some will even match 50% of the employee's contribution, up to a certain limit. Unfortunately, many employees do not value this employer contribution. If you qualify for a 401K at your present place of employment, attend any seminar offered by the company about it. A 401K, for those who qualify, is one of the best opportunities for both reducing current income taxes and supercharging your investment offense.

403B

A 403B is similar to a 401K. Those employed by a tax-exempt religious, charitable or educational organization are eligible to participate in a 403B. The most well-known participants in 403B plans are school teachers. Similar to a 401K, any qualified deductions from salary made to a 403B are not subject to current income taxation. They enjoy current income tax sheltered treatment until withdrawn.

If you think you qualify for a 403B, obtain any information about it from your employer. Most of the monies invested in 403B plans are still in fixed deferred annuities. The number of those investing in 403B plans, through variable deferred annuities, has increased significantly in the past fifteen years. Many of the people who are eligible to participate in a 403B plan do not know that they can also invest their 403B monies in mutual funds. Since 1979, it is not necessary to place these monies in either a fixed or variable deferred annuity. The specific name for this type of mutual fund account is called a 403(b)7. A 403B or 403(b)7 is a powerful current tax reducing strategy and a potentially powerful method of supercharging a person's investment players.

401K AND 403B—DEFINED-CONTRIBUTION PLANS

Both a 401K and 403B are known as defined-contribution plans. The number of defined-contribution plans has increased significantly in the past twenty years. The major reason is the decline of defined benefit-plans. The task of providing for one's retirement is shifting from the employer to the employee. Unlike defined-benefit plans, which require the employer to fully fund and provide a certain pension benefit for employees at retirement, defined-contribution plans—such as a 401K and 403B—place this responsibility square on the shoulders of employees. Fewer and fewer employers are offering defined-benefit plans. They do not want the financial burden that such plans entail. Besides, they can attract and keep qualified employees without offering defined-benefit plans.

SEP-IRA

The administrative work in setting up a 401K plan for employees is elaborate. Recently the paperwork involved has become more streamlined and smaller employers are setting up such plans. Many small employers currently offer a SEP-IRA. SEP-IRA is the acronym for Simplified Employee Pension-Individual Retirement Account. There are certain IRS guidelines that an employer must follow in order to set up a SEP-IRA. The employer makes contributions to the employee's account. The employee may also be allowed to make tax deductible contributions to his or her SEP-IRA account. The employee has control over how the monies in the account are invested.

If you work for an employer that does not have a 401K or SEP-IRA, inquire about the feasibility of setting up such plans. Many small employers are intimidated by the paperwork and responsibility of administering such plans. Some employees are unaware of the potential benefits of these plans and so do not inquire about them. Although all qualified contributions by an employer are a business tax deduction to the employer, many employers believe without investigating further that the costs relative to the benefits are too great. With some basic knowledge and legwork, you may be able to convince your employer otherwise. Self employed individuals that have no employees and partnerships with no employees are also eligible to set up a SEP-IRA plan for themselves.

IRA

Even if you are in your twenties or thirties, do not skip this section just because IRA stands for individual retirement account. An IRA may be a superb vehicle for placing your investment dollars, even if you liquidate all or part of the account before your retirement. Individual Retirement Accounts, commonly called IRAs, were enacted into law by Congress in

1974. Several modifications have been made to this legislation since. The most recent changes were made in 2001. An individual retirement account (IRA) allows those who qualify to place $3,000 (Congress has agreed to incrementally increase this amount—so check for the current figure) each year inside this account. This money is not subject to current income taxation. Today there is great flexibility about the way the monies inside a qualified IRA can be invested.

KEOGH PLAN

Keogh plans are for self-employed individuals. This does not mean that one cannot be an employee and qualify for a Keogh account. As long as a person has a certain amount of self-employment income in a year, he or she can qualify to set up a Keogh account. The qualified contributions made to a Keogh plan are exempt from current income taxation. If a self-employed person has employees, the employees usually have to be included in the plan. The IRS has specific guidelines for this. If you have any self-employment income, you should research further a Keogh account.

TAX DEDUCTIBILITY OF BOTH CONTRIBUTIONS AND INVESTMENT EARNINGS

All the tax sheltered plans reviewed so far—401K, 403B, IRA, SEP-IRA and Keogh—have two important taxation features in common. The qualified contributions to these plans are not subject to current taxation. Second, the investment earnings—capital gains, dividends and interest—are not subject to taxation until withdrawn.

OTHER TAX SHELTERED INVESTMENT PLANS

There are other tax sheltered plans whose contributions do not enjoy income tax deferred treatment but the investment earnings are either tax exempt or sheltered until withdrawn. These are the ones that you should become familiar with now.

DEFERRED ANNUITIES

Non-qualified fixed and variable deferred annuities enjoy tax preferential treatment on their investment earnings until withdrawn. This is one of the features that attracts many people to invest in them. While the tax deferral of investment earnings can be an important consideration in your investment and financial planning, it ought to be evaluated in light of the other strengths and weaknesses of the investment product. Both fixed and variable deferred annuities can be used inside qualified plans, such as an IRA and 403B. Just remember that the contributions to a qualified plan are tax deductible in the year made and the contributions to a non-qualified plan are not. Annuities are reviewed in more detail in Chapter 12.

FIXED AND VARIABLE LIFE INSURANCE

The investment earnings of both fixed and variable whole life and fixed and variable universal life are given tax preferential treatment by the IRS. Their investment earnings are not taxed until withdrawn. That is why many of today's knowledgeable investors are investigating more the positive investment potential of fixed and variable life insurance. This is especially true with respect to variable universal life. As long as Congress continues to give the investment earnings inside fixed and variable life insurance and fixed and variable deferred annuities tax sheltered status, then you will likely see more and more investors look at their investment potential. Fixed and variable life insurance is discussed in greater depth in the next chapter.

NON-DEDUCTIBLE IRA

Most people are not familiar with a non-deductible IRA. The contributions to a non-deductible IRA are not exempt from current income taxation but they are exempt in a qualified IRA. The investment earnings grow income tax deferred inside a non-deductible IRA similar to a deductible IRA.

TAX EXEMPT INVESTMENTS

ROTH IRA

In 1997, Congress passed new legislation affecting IRAs. The most significant change was the introduction of the Roth IRA. The contributions made to a Roth IRA are not tax deductible. But the investment earnings are tax exempt, if the contributions made stay in the account for five years or more. Millions more people can participate in a Roth IRA than in a traditional IRA. The adjusted gross income limitations are higher than for a traditional IRA. Also the fact that a spouse has a qualified retirement plan through work does not preclude his or her spouse from contributing to a Roth IRA.

TAX FAVORED INVESTMENTS

U.S. TREASURIES AND STATE MUNICIPAL BONDS

The federal and state governments have a non-interference policy with respect to taxation of the others debts. The states do not tax the interest earnings on U.S. Treasury bills, Treasury notes and Treasury bonds. This state exemption does not apply to any capital gains made with these debt investments. Likewise, the federal government does not tax the interest earnings on state municipal bonds. It does tax any earned capital gains. Not only does the federal government not tax the interest earnings on state municipal bonds, but the states themselves do not tax the interest earnings on their own state bonds for residents of their state. States do tax the interest earnings on other states municipal bonds. That is why high income taxpayers invest heavily in double-tax-free state municipal bonds. These bonds are tax exempt on their interest earnings at the federal level and also at the state level for people who own bonds that are issued by their state of residence.

RESIDENTIAL REAL ESTATE

Both the federal and state governments offer tax preferential treatment to homeowners. The interest paid, up to a certain amount on a home mortgage loan, is deductible as an itemized deduction on Schedule A of the 1040 Federal Income Tax Form, and it is also deductible on state income taxes, for those states that have a state income tax. This tax preferential treatment of mortgage interest payments, up to the limits allowed by law, plays a significant part in reducing the tax liability of millions of people. Any property taxes paid are also deductible, as an itemized deduction, on Federal Income Taxes. These incentives encourage people to own their own homes. The capital gains attained through the appreciation of owning a home can be postponed indefinitely. In fact, there is a once-in-a-lifetime exclusion of $250,000 ($500,000 per qualified married couple) or less of capital gains for those who are age 55 or over. There are some IRS guidelines that must be met in order to qualify for this exclusion. These tax laws are powerful incentives for millions of people to consider home ownership as a potentially rewarding investment.

SUMMARY

The federal and state governments offer tax incentives to encourage people to invest through specific types of plans. These incentives can range from a current income tax deduction for contributions made to qualified plans to the tax deferral of investment earnings and even tax exemption of investment earnings. They both offer tax incentives to homeowners. Many of these plans are often referred to as retirement accounts. Since they are so often referred to in this manner, many people in their twenties or thirties skip learning about them. If you are in this age category, do not make this error. Thoroughly investigate these plans before you rule out any of them as an intelligent way to achieve your investment and financial goals.

If you are employed by someone else, obtain all the information you can on any investment or so called retirement accounts they offer. Definitely attend any seminars they sponsor on such matters. Do not rule out doing any of this just because you cannot imagine how you could set aside any money right now to invest in them.

YOUR TAX SHELTERED INVESTING GAME PLAN

◆ *Learn the basics about the major tax sheltered plans discussed in this chapter, particularly those you think you might qualify to participate in.*

◆ *Become familiar with the terminology section that follows.* A familiarity with this terminology will help you to more easily understand the investment and financial value of these accounts.

◆ *Find out if your employer sponsors any of these plans.* Also find out if your employer sponsors any other tax sheltered plans not included here. Attend any seminars that your employer sponsors about them. There are very specific IRS guidelines that must be followed by both the employer and employee.

◆ *For a more in-depth knowledge on tax sheltered investing, read* <u>*Getting Started In Tax-Savvy Investing*</u> *by Andrew Westhem and Don Korn.* There is a section at the end where you can mail order this book.

TAX SHELTERED PLANS—TERMINOLOGY

401K Or (Salary Reduction Plan) - It is a company sponsored retirement plan that allows employees to contribute to such a plan on a tax deferred basis. The contributions made by an employee to the plan, up to the limits allowed by law, are not income taxed until withdrawn at a later date. This can be a powerful current income tax reducing strategy. The employee has control over how the monies in his or her 401K are invested. The variety of investment choices available in most 401K plans are many and can be intimidating for many individuals. Every employee, regardless of age, who thinks he or she could qualify to participate in a 401K, should investigate it at his or her place of employment. Once you know the basics about the investment products reviewed in this book, you'll see what a powerful investment and financial planning tool a 401K could be.

403B (Salary Reduction Plan) - A retirement program, similar to a 401K, that is targeted to certain employees. The monies deducted and placed inside a 403B can be invested in deferred annuities and mutual funds. The contributions made, up to the limits allowed by law, are income tax exempt until withdrawn from the plan. Just like a 401K, all interest earnings, dividends and capital gains grow income tax deferred inside a 403B until withdrawn.

Defined-Contribution Pension Plan - A pension plan that employees can contribute to. The benefits vary according to a specific formula. The amount paid out at retirement is not guaranteed. It depends on how the monies in the plan were invested and how well or poorly they performed. Some examples of defined-contribution plans are 401Ks and 403Bs.

Exempt Income - Certain income that is not taxed. Interest income from state municipal bonds is neither taxed by the federal government or by the state government to the residents of the state that own such bonds. States tax the interest income on any of their residents who receive state municipal bond interest from other state bonds.

Individual Retirement Account Plan (IRA) - A tax deferred plan that allows certain individuals to place $3,000 or maybe more each year in an IRA. This money is exempt from current income taxation. Also, all interest earnings, dividends and capital gains achieved inside an IRA are exempt from current income taxation until withdrawn later. Like a 401K or 403B, the investment options available with IRAs are numerous.

Itemized Deductions - Deductions made on a specific federal income tax form called Schedule A. If a person's itemized deductions are greater than their standard deduction, he or she can deduct from their adjusted gross income whichever one is greater, to arrive at his or her taxable income. Mortgage interest is deductible as an itemized deduction on Schedule A of Federal Income Tax Form 1040.

Keogh Pension Plan (HR-10) - A tax deferred plan for those individuals who have self employment income. The contributions, up to the limits allowed by law, made to such a plan are income tax deductible until withdrawn. Certain employees must be included in a Keogh plan.

Mortgage Interest Deduction - Interest paid on a mortgage loan for a home purchase is deductible on a persons federal income tax return. It is called an itemized deduction on Schedule A of Form 1040. Currently, a couple filing jointly can deduct the interest on a mortgage loan for their principal residence, up to $1 million dollars. The mortgage interest tax deduction is a significant tax savings for millions of people.

Municipal Bond Interest Or (Munee Bond Interest) - The U.S. Government does not tax interest earnings on state municipal bonds. Neither do the states tax the interest earnings on their own state municipal bonds. Often you will hear the phrase—invest in double-tax-free state municipal bonds. There are now many mutual funds that invest exclusively in double-tax-free state municipal bonds. Generally, it is high income tax rate payers that invest in double-tax-free state municipal bonds.

Roth IRA (Individual Retirement Account) - An account whose investment earnings are not just tax deferred but also tax exempt, if held in the plan for over five years. There is no income tax deduction allowed for contributions made to a Roth IRA. Millions more taxpayers can qualify to contribute to a Roth IRA than a traditional IRA for two reasons. First, the adjusted gross income threshold is much higher with a Roth IRA than a traditional IRA. Second, a person can contribute to a Roth IRA even if his or her spouse has a pension plan through work.

SEP IRA (Simplified Employee Pension Plan) - Many small employers set up SEP IRA plans for their employees. The administrative work is much more streamlined compared to a 401K plan. The contributions to a SEP IRA are funded by contributions from the employer. An arrangement can be set up whereby the employee can contribute to a SEP IRA through the employer. Contributions to a SEP IRA are deductible to the employer as an expense item.

Tax Deferral - A feature available with many investment plans that allows for contributions to be income tax deferred until withdrawn. The interest earnings, dividends and capital gains may also be tax deferred until withdrawn. Examples of such tax deferred plans are 401Ks, 403Bs, IRAs and Keogh plans. Good tax planning is a very important component for becoming a star quarterback of your investment plan.

Tax Exempt Income - Certain income that is exempt from federal or state income taxes or both. Municipal bond interest can be exempt from both federal and state income taxes. Investment earnings in a Roth IRA, if kept in the account for at least five years, is exempt from federal income taxation.

CHAPTER
◆ 11 ◆

FIXED AND VARIABLE LIFE INSURANCE

Protect Your Investment Offense

In the "Game Plan" section of the previous chapters, I've recommended that you learn the terminology particular to that topic and investment player—after you have read the chapter. But in this chapter, I recommend a slightly different strategy. You should focus on understanding key life insurance terms from the outset—not later. It's much easier to get quickly confused and abandon the idea of understanding life insurance, as an investment, than stocks, bonds, money market securities, savings accounts and mutual funds. You needn't let the relative complexity of this hybrid investment discourage you from trying to understand its basics, as long as you've got a firm grasp on the fundamentals of the major investment players.

RALPH NADER IS DEAD WRONG

The reason for confusion and apprehension among consumers about life insurance eludes most financial writers and commentators, including

Ralph Nader and Wesley Smith. In *Winning The Insurance Game*, Nader and Smith state that just the "very mention of the subject [life insurance] drains the color from one's face."

If the morbidity of contemplating our own death causes most of us to recoil from trying to understand and make wise decisions about life insurance, why then does the mere thought of going to a dealership to buy a car "drain the color" from most people's faces? It is certainly not the "morbidity of the subject." In fact, if you stop and analyze it, you'll discover that the color drains from most people's faces for exactly the same reasons when they think about either buying life insurance or buying a car from a dealer. Ralph Nader and Wesley Smith are dead wrong—the thought of one's death, untimely or otherwise, is not one of the major reasons. Nader and Smith fail to address the average consumer's lack of insurance knowledge as being the primary cause that "drains the color" from people's faces.

CAR BUYING—AN ANALOGY

Many people enter a dealership to purchase a car with little knowledge of four important particulars:

> ➢ what the dealer paid for the car they want to buy
> ➢ what specific options they want and what the dealer paid for those options
> ➢ how they are going to finance the car loan at the best prevailing interest rate
> ➢ the wholesale value of their trade-in vehicle

Since many car buyers are uninformed about these four essentials, the salesperson can easily pull the wool over their eyes. These salespeople only look so "good" because the "competition" is poorly prepared. The old adage, "knowledge is power" certainly applies to buying a car.

SIMILARLY WITH FIXED AND VARIABLE LIFE INSURANCE

There are three important features about fixed and variable life insurance that most people are uninformed about:

> the mortality costs of the policy
> the investment portion of the contract
> the up-front and ongoing costs associated with purchasing and managing the policy

If a potential buyer is uninformed about any one of these areas, not to mention all three, the insurance agent or financial planner can, like the auto salesperson, use smoke and mirror sales tactics with the prospective client. They can make exaggerated and untruthful claims about the product with impunity. By mastering some basic life insurance terminology right now, you can level this "playing field" in a hurry and eliminate any apprehension you may have about examining this financial product.

THE BEGINNING OF KNOWLEDGE

The most important terms you should become familiar with right now are:

> term life
> fixed life
> variable life
> whole life
> universal life
> subaccount (or separate account)
> surrender charge
> mortality charge
> expense charges
> commission (or load)

TERM LIFE INSURANCE

Until about the middle of the nineteenth century, only one type of life insurance policy was sold—*term life insurance*. This policy had just a death benefit. It did not have any cash value, savings or investment feature and so it was very easy to understand. It paid a certain amount of money, called the "face amount" of the policy, to the named beneficiary on the death of the insured person. That was it.

This same policy is sold today and it is called *term life insurance.* There are several types of term life policies. The most common are known as *annual renewal term* (ART), *level term* and *decreasing term.* None of them have an investment component. The main focus in the rest of this chapter will therefore be on the investment potential of fixed and variable life insurance, because these policies have an investment feature coupled with life insurance protection.

If you want to comparison-shop the rates on various term life insurance policies, you should read product reviews in *Consumer Reports* magazine. To identify relevant issues with insurance reviews, look up "insurance" in *Consumer Report's* comprehensive subject index, available in the reference section of your public library. You can also call *Consumer Reports* at 800-766-9988 to order their back issues on term life insurance . The cost is minuscule in relation to the value of the information contained in this publication. You can also call Select Quote at 800-343-1985 for the rates on some of the most competitive term life policies.

FIXED AND VARIABLE WHOLE LIFE INSURANCE

In the middle of the nineteenth century, some life insurance companies added a new feature to one of their term life policies—a cash value buildup. The cash value feature was added to the insurance company's decreasing term policy. The premium on this policy remained the same for the duration of the contract. The interest rate credited to the cash value, or investment portion of the policy, also remained fixed for the duration of the contract.

FIXED WHOLE LIFE

This policy was called a fixed whole life policy, although the word "fixed" was not usually used to describe it. A portion of the premium went to pay for the death benefit and a portion went to the cash value buildup. The portion that went to the death benefit was greater than actuarially necessary during the early years of the policy. This was done in order to make the premium affordable during the latter years of the contract.

Fixed whole life had three major drawbacks. There was no flexibility in premium payments, regardless of a person's financial circumstances. It was an inflexible product in responding to financial market conditions; the interest rate credited to the cash value or investment portion of the contract always remained the same. Financial returns were very poor over the long-term, compared to other investments. In fact, the Federal Trade Commission reported in 1979 that fixed whole life insurance policies usually only produced about a 2% to 4% return, even when the policies remained in force for over twenty years.

VARIABLE WHOLE LIFE

The Equitable Life Assurance Company introduced a new whole life policy in 1976. It was called "variable whole life". This was a revolutionary new product for a financial institution as conservative as the life insurance industry. Securities were bought and sold for almost two hundred years prior to 1976, but this was the first time they were linked with life insurance. Similar to a fixed whole life policy, the premiums remained level throughout the contract. But unlike the fixed whole life policy, the owner had control over the investment portion or what was called the investment subaccount and how the monies in it were invested. In spite of the very positive results produced over the next several years, sales of these contracts were dismal in comparison to fixed whole life.

It took a different financial climate for variable securities linked with life insurance to increase in popularity. This climate occurred in the late 1970s and early 1980s. Two new life insurance policies—fixed universal life insurance and variable universal life insurance—were developed during this period.

FIXED AND VARIABLE UNIVERSAL LIFE

If you have forgotten what money market securities and mutual funds are, or skipped Chapter 7 and 8, return to them now before proceeding any further. You will understand the investment potential of fixed and variable life insurance much more easily if you know the basics about money market securities, savings accounts and mutual funds.

The factor that forced the life insurance industry to develop both fixed and variable universal life insurance was the historically high interest rates that were paid on money market securities during the late 1970s and early 1980s. During this time period, Merrill Lynch and other brokerage companies developed money market mutual funds. Shortly thereafter, banks and savings and loans started money market deposit accounts. Both of these events allowed millions of people the opportunity to invest in money market securities with relatively small amounts of money. Prior to this, money market securities were off limits to small investors due to the high amounts of money needed to invest in them directly.

With the development of these two new investment products—money market mutual funds and money market deposit accounts—billions of dollars poured out of life insurance policies and into these accounts. People borrowed billions from their fixed whole life policies at 5% and reinvested those monies in money market deposit accounts and money market mutual funds and earned anywhere from 8% to 18% annually during the late 1970s and early 1980s.

FIXED UNIVERSAL LIFE

In a traditional fixed whole life policy, the interest rate is set at the beginning of the contract and never changes during the policy period. This was not the case with the newly developed fixed universal life policy. The interest rate was fixed, but only for a short period, such as three months, six months, a year or at some other time interval. The interest rate paid fluctuates with current financial market conditions.

Generally, the interest rate paid on fixed universal life policies is a little higher than money market rates. It is very similar to the rates paid on fixed deferred annuities, which will be discussed in the next chapter. Therefore, if you want the purchasing power of your invested dollars to grow significantly over time beyond the inflation rate, you'd better look elsewhere rather than fixed universal life insurance. Two places to look could be variable universal life insurance and variable deferred annuities.

Unlike both fixed and variable whole life insurance, you can opt for flexible premium payments with both fixed or variable universal life insurance. Flexibility in premium payments is an important feature to have in your life insurance and investment program.

VARIABLE UNIVERSAL LIFE INSURANCE

Variable universal life insurance, in the investment portion of the contract, operates very similar to a mutual fund. There is a subaccount for the investment portion of the plan. The subaccount monies are not co-mingled with the other monies of the life insurance company. The policyholder owns and controls the subaccount. Although the amount of investment choices in a variable universal life subaccount are not usually as extensive as a typical mutual fund, they are nevertheless very significant and of course much greater than with fixed universal life.

The investment options available in variable universal life subaccounts are increasing every year and will likely continue to do so. Like a mutual fund, you can invest in a variable universal life subaccount that consists of money market securities, bonds and stocks. You can also invest in subaccounts that focus on specific sectors of these three broad investment categories.

The subaccount contains an insurance feature similar to the insurance or death guarantee in the subaccount of a variable deferred annuity. This death benefit, for which there is a premium or mortality charge, simply guarantees that in the event of the insured's death during the policy contract, the beneficiary will receive either the amount of monies invested in the subaccount or its market value, whichever is greater at the time of death.

TAXATION OF INVESTMENT EARNINGS

The investment earnings—interest, capital gains and dividends—achieved with fixed and variable life insurance, grow tax deferred until withdrawn.

On withdrawal, investment earnings are taxed at income tax rates rather than the long-term capital gains rate. The long-term capital gains rate could be lower or higher than a person's income tax rate when withdrawing money from these policies. Therefore, you need to evaluate the tax consequences before investing in either fixed or variable life insurance.

It is also worth noting that on the insured's death, the beneficiary will not have to pay income taxes on the life insurance proceeds, including the investment earnings. The value of the contract, however, is considered part of the contract owner's estate and is taxed accordingly on the death of the named insured. The exclusion of life insurance proceeds from taxation, for the beneficiary, can be an important positive feature of this product.

SURRENDER CHARGES

You will usually have to pay high surrender charges with fixed and variable life insurance, if you cancel the policy during the early years of the contract. Customarily, policies purchased directly from a company rather than through sales representatives will have less severe surrender charges. The surrender charges are usually on a sliding scale and normally disappear between the fifth and tenth year of the contract.

MORTALITY COSTS

Life insurance companies are now required to disclose their mortality costs to prospective buyers. Having said that, it is still not easy for beginners to comparison-shop the cost of the life insurance part of the policy. This task is easier than it has been in the past for those who are Internet savvy.

EXPENSE CHARGES

There are several expense costs with both fixed and variable life insurance. These are the most common:

> ➢ *Policy fee.* Most insurance companies charge a fee for initiating a policy.

> *Sales charge or load.* Fixed life insurance is sold without any sales charge. Variable life may be sold with or without a sales charge. With variable life, the prospectus will spell out if there is any load and if so how much. Regardless of whether there is or is not a sales load with these policies, you should be aware of any surrender charges and for how long they last.

> *Management fee.* Fixed life has no management fee but it usually has an annual maintenance charge. Variable life charges a management fee and it can range anywhere from .3% to 3% of the policy's subaccount market value. This management fee is assessed annually.

INVESTMENT RETURNS

If you know how to evaluate the investment potential of stocks, bonds, money market securities, savings accounts and mutual funds, you will be able to easily assess the likely investment returns from fixed and variable life insurance. Just like savings accounts and money market securities, you should only expect short investment yardage gains with fixed life insurance, even over the long-term. You certainly can expect to achieve long investment yardage gains with variable universal life if you keep mortality costs and expense charges to a competitive minimum, and you are willing to invest in common stocks for the long haul.

HOW TO IDENTIFY YOUR MVP

What you have read in this chapter is just an introduction to fixed and variable whole life and fixed and variable universal life insurance. It is important to understand some basic terminology about these products before reading more complex discussions of them.

As your basic knowledge of the investment players reviewed in this book grows, you will find that variable universal life will be your product of choice from this chapter—your MVP—Most Valuable Player. Variable universal life, unlike fixed and variable whole life and fixed universal life, places the most control in your hands. It offers you control over the life insurance amount, the premium payments and the investment options. This amount of control can be very intimidating to the uninformed investor, but once you know the fundamentals about the major investment players—you will want to have as much control and flexibility as possible over your investment choices.

YOUR LIFE INSURANCE INVESTING GAME PLAN

◗ *Become familiar with several fixed and variable life insurance terms at the outset to avoid feeling overwhelmed.* The most important terms to know right now are:

➢ fixed life insurance

➢ variable life insurance

➢ term life insurance

➢ whole life insurance

➢ universal life insurance

➢ subaccount (or separate account)

➢ surrender charge

➢ mortality and expense charges

➢ commission or load

◗ *Investigate the following three areas in order to assess the suitability of buying fixed or variable life insurance:*

a) the mortality costs of each policy.

b) the expenses and administrative costs—if any—associated with each plan.

c) the investment returns of each plan over the long-term.

◗ *Make sure you have understood the basics about stocks, bonds, money market securities, savings accounts and mutual funds before reading this chapter on fixed and variable life insurance.*

◗ *If you need life insurance protection right now but do not feel knowledgeable enough to evaluate fixed and variable life insurance, you should purchase a term life policy that has an option of converting it later to either a fixed or variable life policy.* Back issues of *Consumer Reports* magazines on life insurance can be very helpful in making an intelligent decision in this area. A company called Select Quote at 800-343-1985 will provide rates on some of the most competitive term life insurance policies.

- *Read whatever comparison information exists.* Key sources to check are:

  - ➤ *Consumer Reports* magazine for their collected information on these products.

  - ➤ *Barrons* weekly newspaper for comparison data on variable life. It has a page with data on several variable life policies and their investment returns.

  - ➤ *How to Read the Financial Pages* by Peter Passell will prepare you for comparison shopping with the data on variable able life insurance in *Barrons* weekly newspaper. *How to Read the Financial Pages* is recommended in Chapter 13 "Understanding the Economic News."

- *Read the first twelve chapters of* <u>*The New Life Insurance Investment Advisor*</u> *by Ben Baldwin.*

FIXED AND VARIABLE LIFE INSURANCE — TERMINOLOGY

Accumulation Account - A term used in universal life insurance that describes all the total premiums paid and interest credited to the account, before any deductions for life insurance, expenses, loans or surrenders.

Actuary - A person who calculates the statistical probability of certain events occurring for insurance companies and others. Examples of such events are fires, auto accidents, death rates for men and women of certain ages and for specific causes.

Cash Surrender Value - The amount of money a person receives on surrendering their cash value life policy. Any surrender charges and outstanding loans are deducted first from the cash value to arrive at the net Cash Surrender Value.

Cash Value Life Policy - A life insurance policy that has a cash value as well as a death benefit. The amount of the cash value varies from policy to policy. It depends on the amount of interest paid and investment earnings on the cash value portion of the plan. Term life insurance does not have any cash value.

Fixed Life Insurance - A cash value life policy that pays a set interest rate for a specified period. The interest rate could change every three months, six months, a year or at some other interval. Even though the interest rate can change periodically, it is still called Fixed Life Insurance.

Fixed Universal Life Insurance - A cash value life policy with an interest rate that fluctuates periodically. The amount of life insurance can vary and so can the premium. This is a more flexible life policy than a fixed whole life policy and it is also more responsive to current market conditions.

Fixed Whole Life Insurance - A cash value life policy with a set interest rate for the life of the plan. Both the life insurance amount and the premium amount also remain fixed.

Mortality and Expense Charges (M&E) - These are charges made against the market value of the subaccount in variable life insurance. M&E Charges pay for the insurance feature and other expenses in variable life. The prospectus specifies the amount of these charges. Examine them closely to avoid being gouged. Some insurance companies are charging enormous M&E fees.

Scheduled Premium Variable Life Insurance - Equitable Life Assurance introduced a variable life policy to the market in 1976. It featured fixed premiums and a fixed amount of life insurance; however, for the first time, insurance had a subaccount or separate account that invested in securities. This subaccount or separate account operated similarly to a mutual fund. The policy owner had a choice of investment options.

Subaccount or Separate Account - An account in variable life insurance that operates similar to a mutual fund. The owner has control over how the monies in this Subaccount are invested. Currently there are many investment options in most variable life insurance Subaccounts.

Surrender Charge - Life insurance companies levy this fee, for the surrender of a cash value life policy. This Surrender Charge varies from company to company and is usually on a sliding scale. The Surrender Charge typically disappears between the fifth and tenth year of the policy.

Term Life Insurance - Sometimes referred to as pure life insurance. Term Life Insurance has no cash value. There are many kinds of term life policies. The most common are annual renewal term, decreasing term and level term. Many companies offer term life policies to age 95. It is an excellent plan for people who need a lot of life insurance protection, but have limited financial resources.

Universal Life Insurance - Universal Life Insurance comes in two varieties—fixed and variable. Universal Life is much more responsive to current market conditions, compared to fixed whole life insurance. Unlike fixed whole life, Universal Life Insurance offers flexibility in premium payments, death protection and investment options.

Variable Life Insurance - Unlike fixed whole life or fixed universal life, the investment monies in Variable Life Insurance are not comingled with the other monies of the life insurance company. Instead, they are placed in a separate account or subaccount. The policyholder owns this subaccount and has control at all times over how the monies in it are invested. Today, there are many investment options that a person can select with most Variable Life policies.

Whole Life - A cash value life policy. The premium and face value remain the same for the life of the policy. This was the most popular form of life policy sold during the past one hundred and fifty years. Knowledgeable investors usually consider other investment alternatives to Whole Life Insurance.

CHAPTER
✦ 12 ✦

FIXED
AND VARIABLE
ANNUITIES

Guard Your Investment Offense

Just as beginning investors may feel tempted to throw in the towel on understanding fixed and variable life insurance, so too may they feel stymied by annuities. But those who become familiar with certain annuity terminology at the outset should find these investments easier to understand and evaluate than fixed and variable life insurance. The important terms are:

- ➤ annuity
- ➤ annuitize
- ➤ immediate annuity
- ➤ deferred annuity
- ➤ fixed deferred annuity
- ➤ variable deferred annuity
- ➤ subaccount (or separate account)
- ➤ surrender charge

The word annuity evolved from the Latin word annus, which means year and alludes to the annual payment a life insurance company makes to a designated beneficiary.

Annuities are easier to understand and evaluate, compared to fixed and variable life insurance, because they are almost exclusively investment products. Legally, only life insurance companies can sell annuities, which leads many people to assume that they are mainly insurance products. Therefore, many overlook their investment potential. In fact, only variable deferred annuities have an insurance feature—and it is a very minor one at that.

WHY SOLD ONLY BY INSURANCE COMPANIES?

If annuities are almost exclusively investments, why then are they only sold through life insurance companies? No logical explanation exists, as far as I know. The sole reason I can fathom is the political clout of the life insurance industry. That is the present reality. Therefore, do not let this fact preclude you from reading up on the investment potential of annuities. The lack of readily available inexpensive data sources to comparison-shop annuities in such financial magazines as *Worth, Forbes, Money, Kiplinger's* and other financial publications may also discourage people from considering annuities.

There is also a third factor that causes people to pull back from analyzing the investment potential of annuities. It is the confusion in many people's minds, and this even includes otherwise very knowledgeable investors, regarding the major difference between an immediate and deferred annuity. Let's start by first getting a clear picture of what an annuity is.

WHAT IS AN ANNUITY?

With an annuity, a person deposits a certain sum of money with a life insurance company and designates a beneficiary in the annuity contract. Then the insurance company pays the beneficiary annually, or at some other agreed upon interval. The payments will be made for the remainder of the annuitant's life, or some other period.

Possibly 80% to 90% of the annuities in existence today are not annuities by the definition just given. Why not? Because some financial products, while retaining their original names, have evolved over time to be different from what they began as. Yes—you can purchase today an annuity similar to the description just stated. This kind of an annuity is called an "immediate annuity."

The most popular type of an annuity invested in today is called a "deferred annuity." It is not really an annuity at all. Nonetheless, as a beginning investor, you should become knowledgeable about deferred annuities. We'll first briefly review immediate annuities so that you have at least a basic idea of their investment potential.

WHAT IS AN IMMEDIATE ANNUITY?

In an immediate annuity contract, a life insurance company agrees that on receiving a certain amount of money, the company will make payments to the beneficiary annually (or at some other agreed upon interval) for a designated period, such as the remainder of the annuitant's life.

Annuitizing a sum of money with a life insurance company can be an intelligent investment choice for some people. Once a person annuitizes a sum of money with a life insurance company, neither party can change the contract later. Therefore, investors should be knowledgeable about annuitization options before committing their money to any of them.

THREE ANNUITIZATION OPTIONS

Think of annuitizing a sum of money with a life insurance company as an investment decision and not an insurance decision. Do you recall my definition of an investment in Chapter 2? It is an expenditure of money with the expectation of obtaining a greater financial return in the future.

FIRST ANNUITIZATION OPTION

Take, for example, a single person who has retired from the workforce. Besides her Social Security and pension check, she has $200,000 in certificates of deposit. She is considering annuitizing this $200,000 with a life insurance company. She is 65 years of age, has no dependents and is mainly concerned about providing herself with as high a monthly income as realistically possible for the rest of her life. She is therefore considering a straight life annuitization option.

If she selects this annuitization option and one year later dies, the life insurance company will only have paid out say $18,000 dollars or $1,500 a month. Under this annuitization option, the life insurance company is not obligated to pay any more money. If, on the other hand, she lives to age 100 and the insurance company has agreed to pay her $1,500 a month, then they will pay her a total of $630,000. If she selects any other annuitization option, besides a straight life annuitization option, she will receive less than $1,500 a month.

This type of an annuity, where the payout is set at the same amount each month or at some other interval, is called a fixed immediate annuity. A person could select an annuitization option where the payment can change each month. This type of immediate annuity is called a variable immediate annuity. You met both of these words "fixed" and "variable" in the last chapter on fixed and variable life insurance. They represent certain methods of investing through life insurance and annuities.

SECOND ANNUITIZATION EXAMPLE

In this scenario, a husband and wife have just turned 65 and retired from the work force. Usually this is a time when many people closely review their investment and financial situation and make many decisions.

Our retired couple have their Social Security and pension checks, and $400,000 in certificates of deposit. They have read up on various annuitization options and are drawn to one called a "joint and survivor life immediate annuity." It is a fixed immediate annuity.

Here's how this annuitization option works. The insurance company pays out until both of them die. The payment can be the same, even if one of them dies, or they can structure it so that the survivor receives 50% of what both were receiving prior to the death of one of them.

In each of these two annuitization examples, the people are trying to maximize the amount they receive monthly, for as long as they live. They are not concerned about leaving anyone else any money. Some people should consider this type of annuitization option. It can be a very intelligent investment choice.

THIRD ANNUITIZATION EXAMPLE

One more annuitization example and you should have a basic idea how annuitizing a sum of money with a life insurance company works. Make a mental note to read more about annuitization options and immediate annuities in the books I've recommended later in this chapter.

This annuitization option is called "a life annuity with a period certain." This period could be ten or twenty years, for instance. The first annuitization option does not appeal to some people for this reason: if the annuitant dies three months after annuitization has occurred, the life insurance company is not legally required to pay out any more money.

Let us imagine this scenario is exactly the same as the first example, but the person wants the life insurance company to pay out a monthly amount for ten years, no matter if the annuitant dies at any time before these ten years are past. The annuitant dies after one year. Then the annuity payments are made to the beneficiary for the balance of the ten years. If this is the annuitization option selected, then you certainly know that the insurance company will pay out less than $1,500 a month. Under this annuitization option, they may only agree to pay out $1,200 a month.

These are but three examples of annuitization options. There are many more kinds of annuitization choices. Reading up on all these annuitization options in one sitting can be very confusing and counterproductive. For now, just get a clear idea what annuitizing a sum of money with a life insurance company means. Later, you can read more on this area of investing through annuities.

Let's look at the area of annuity investing that you should become most familiar with now: deferred annuities.

WHAT IS A DEFERRED ANNUITY?

A deferred annuity is technically not an annuity. It is basically an investment that is given income tax sheltered treatment. The tax preferential treatment enjoyed by deferred annuities is the major reason why many people invest through this financial product. If you recall the definition of an annuity stated earlier, a deferred annuity is not a true annuity. The only true annuity is an immediate annuity. In other words, a sum of money has been annuitized with a life insurance company. Deferred annuities have not gone through this annuitization process. Annuitizing a deferred annuity is an option. Most people who own deferred annuities do not plan to annuitize the monies in these accounts. They invest through them mainly because the investment earnings grow income tax deferred until withdrawn.

FIXED AND VARIABLE DEFERRED ANNUITIES

There are two ways of investing in deferred annuities. One method is through fixed deferred annuities and the other is through variable deferred annuities.

FIXED DEFERRED ANNUITY

A fixed deferred annuity pays a set interest rate on the principal invested for a specific period of time, such as three months, six months, a year or some other time interval. Once an annuity earns interest, this interest is added to the principal and interest is then paid on the principal plus the interest earned. This is called compound interest. The interest rate paid depends on prevailing market conditions and the insurance company. The interest rate paid on fixed deferred annuities is usually a little higher than average money market rates. Therefore, if it is important that the purchasing power of your invested dollars increase significantly over time, then you should consider investing in something other than fixed deferred annuities.

Think of a fixed deferred annuity as a debt investment. With this investment, a person is lending his or her money to a life insurance company and getting paid interest for doing so. It is similar to a fixed life insurance policy or a certificate of deposit. A certificate of deposit at a bank or savings and loan does not enjoy income tax preferential treatment on its interest earnings, while the IRS treats the investment earnings of both fixed and variable life and fixed and variable deferred annuities preferentially.

The principal—the amount invested in a fixed deferred annuity—is guaranteed to be returned at any time. Just be sure that A.M. Best and Standard and Poor's rate the life insurance company as financially strong. With a strongly rated, fixed deferred annuity, you can be confident that your principal (less any surrender charge) will be returned upon request.

VARIABLE DEFERRED ANNUITY

Variable deferred annuities could be the solution to the relatively slower growth that your dollar earns in a fixed deferred annuity. A variable deferred annuity operates similarly to a mutual fund. Just as you can own shares in a mutual fund, you own and control the subaccount in a variable deferred annuity. The money invested in the subaccount is not commingled with the other monies of the life insurance company. The market value of this subaccount can fluctuate daily, depending upon the kind of securities—such as stocks, bonds and money market securities—in which they are invested. Once you know the basics of how to invest through mutual funds, you will easily know how you can invest in the subaccount of a variable deferred annuity. Other major features that you should be aware of about investing through fixed and variable deferred annuities are discussed in the next several paragraphs.

TAXATION OF INVESTMENT EARNINGS

The investment earnings (interest, capital gains and dividends) grow tax deferred inside the subaccount of a variable deferred annuity. The interest earnings in fixed deferred annuities also grow income tax deferred until withdrawn. This tax deferral of investment earnings is the major feature that attracts millions of people to invest through deferred annuities. The investment earnings of mutual funds, unless they are sheltered inside some form of a qualified retirement account, are subject to current income taxation. Investment earnings of both fixed and variable deferred annuities are taxed upon withdrawal at income tax rates and not at the long-term capital gains rate.

SURRENDER CHARGES

Most insurance companies do not charge sales or commission fees on the principal invested in either fixed or variable deferred annuities. They do impose surrender charges if the policies are surrendered or cancelled before a certain time has elapsed. The surrender period and the amount of surrender charges varies from company to company. Investigate this surrender period and the surrender charges before deciding which insurance company to invest through.

Most insurance companies allow an investor to withdraw a certain amount of the principal each year (usually 10%), without imposing any surrender charges. Think of these surrender charges as similar to the penalty charges imposed by banks and savings and loans on the early withdrawal or surrender of certificates of deposit.

IRS PENALTY ON EARLY WITHDRAWAL OF INVESTMENT EARNINGS

The government offers income tax preferential treatment on the investment earnings in both fixed and variable deferred annuities. Part of the reason they receive this tax deferred preferential treatment is to encourage people to invest for their retirement. Consequently, the IRS charges a 10% penalty on any investment earnings withdrawn from either fixed or variable deferred annuities before age $59^1/_2$.

ONGOING DEFERRED ANNUITY CHARGES

There are no ongoing charges assessed against fixed deferred annuities. The charges assessed against the subaccount in a variable deferred annuity can be significant. Again, you should analyze these charges before investing.

Just because there are no ongoing charges assessed against fixed deferred annuities does not mean that they are a better investment than variable deferred annuities.

Remember that the interest paid on fixed deferred annuities is usually just a little higher than that paid on money market securities. Therefore, don't count on the purchasing power of your invested monies increasing much with fixed deferred annuities.

KEY CHARGES IN VARIABLE DEFERRED ANNUITIES

A. MORTALITY AND EXPENSE CHARGES (M AND E)

Variable deferred annuities have a mortality charge. This mortality charge is made for the life insurance feature in this investment product. If the annuitant dies during the contract period, the beneficiary receives either the value of all the monies deposited in the subaccount or the market value of the subaccount, whichever is greater.

The mortality charge for this ever-so-minor life insurance feature can be expensive. Several insurance companies have been reducing this mortality charge in order to encourage more people to invest through their variable deferred annuities. Included with this mortality charge are other expense charges. They are combined together and assessed as a percentage amount, such as 1% or 2% of the subaccount's market value. This M and E charge is assessed against the subaccount's market value annually.

B. MANAGEMENT FEE

This is a percent charge assessed annually against a variable deferred annuity's subaccount market value for management of the account. This annual percentage charge could be a high as 3% to 4%. Many investors don't get sufficient bang for their buck in this area of investing. Investigate closely the management fee charge. It will be stated in the variable annuity prospectus. Just like mutual funds, variable annuities must be sold with a prospectus. The prospectus will state all the various charges assessed. Analyze them closely. Over many years of investing, the management fee and other charges can add up to be a very significant amount.

C. ANNUAL MAINTENANCE CHARGE

Many insurance companies assess an annual maintenance charge of about $30 on each variable deferred annuity.

SUMMARY

Both fixed and variable deferred annuities can play an intelligent role in many people's investment planning. Their major attraction is the tax preferential treatment given to their investment earnings until withdrawn. The major drawback of fixed deferred annuities is their relatively low investment returns over the long run. The investment returns over the short and long-term usually just exceed money market securities. If it is important that the purchasing power of your invested dollars increase significantly beyond the rate of inflation, then you should look at investments other than fixed deferred annuities. Variable deferred annuities could be the answer to that challenge. The major drawback of most variable deferred annuities are the high account charges assessed against the subaccount's market value annually. It is crucial to examine these subaccount charges before investing. Not all insurance companies levy the same amount.

There are two ways of investing in deferred annuities. One is with a fixed deferred annuity, where the insurance company pays a specific interest rate for a specified period of time, such as three months, six months, one year or five years. The rate paid fluctuates according to prevailing market conditions. This rate is usually a little higher than average money market rates.

The second way of investing is through variable deferred annuities. With a variable deferred annuity, the investor owns and controls the investment subaccount. The investor can easily change investment strategy in this subaccount according to his or her goals and how he or she perceives general market conditions.

To boost your knowledge of fixed and variable annuities, read Chapter 13 titled "Understanding Annuities" in *The New Life Insurance Investment Advisor* by Ben Baldwin and also *Getting Started In Annuities* by Gordon Williamson.

YOUR FIXED AND VARIABLE ANNUITY GAME PLAN

⬤ *Get to know some basic annuity terminology before you read more in-depth on this tax sheltered investment product.* The following are the most important terms to know now:

➢ Annuity
➢ Annuitize
➢ Immediate annuity
➢ Deferred annuity
➢ Fixed deferred annuity
➢ Variable deferred annuity
➢ Subaccount (sometimes called a separate account)
➢ Surrender charge

⬤ *Make sure you have read and understood the basics about stocks, bonds, money market securities, savings accounts and mutual funds before working with this chapter.* By pursuing this strategy you will easily understand how to invest through fixed and variable deferred annuities.

⬤ *After you have read the book* How To Read The Financial Pages *(which is recommended in the chapter, "Understanding The Economic News"), particularly the section on mutual funds, read the data page in* Barron's weekly Newspaper on variable deferred annuities. You can obtain a copy of Barron's weekly newspaper at your local library or major book store.

⬤ *For a more in-depth understanding of the investment and other financial potential of fixed and variable annuities read:*
a) Chapter 13 in *The New Life Insurance Investment Advisor* by Ben Baldwin. It is titled "Understanding Annuities."
b) *Getting Started In Annuities* by Gordon Williamson.

Also, consult the section at the end of this book to find out how to mail order these books.

ANNUITIES—TERMINOLOGY

Accumulation Period - The period of time during which the principal, interest earnings and capital gains grow tax deferred inside a deferred annuity.

Annuitize - The process of drawing up an agreement between one or more people and a life insurance company for the payment annually (or at some other interval), to a beneficiary named in the contract for the remainder of the annuitant's life or for a certain period on depositing a sum of money with that life insurance company.

Annuity - The payment annually or at another interval made by a life insurance company to a designated beneficiary for the remainder of the annuitant's life or for a certain period.

Bail-Out Provision - A provision that is usually offered with a fixed deferred annuity. When the renewal interest rate paid is less by 1% or more of the rate previously paid, the annuity owner can liquidate all or part of the contract without any cost, fee or penalty. There is an IRS penalty of 10% on any interest earnings.

Deferred Annuity - An investment product that includes tax deferred treatment on its investment earnings among some of its characteristics. Earnings are not taxed until withdrawn. Deferred annuities are technically not annuities. They have not been annuitized. Annuitizing a deferred annuity is an option, not a requirement. Most deferred annuities are never annuitized.

Fixed Deferred Annuity - A fixed deferred annuity pays a set interest rate on the monies invested, for a specific period of time. This time period could be three months, six months, a year, five years or some other interval. The interest rate paid on fixed deferred annuities usually fluctuates with market conditions. If the Federal Reserve Board increases short-term interest rates, then life insurance companies are likely to increase the interest rate paid on their fixed deferred annuities. Likewise, if the Federal Reserve Board decreases short-term interest rates, then life insurance companies will likely reduce the interest rate they pay on their fixed deferred annuities.

Immediate Annuity - An annuitized sum of money. An Immediate Annuity is an agreement between an individual and a life insurance company for the pay-out of certain sums of money at agreed on intervals, subsequent to that person depositing a specific sum of money with the life insurance company.

Single Premium Deferred Annuity (SPDA) - Most deferred annuities are invested in over a period of time, usually on a monthly basis. Some individuals, because of financial circumstances, may decide to set up a deferred annuity with a lump sum of money and not make any other contributions. This kind of annuity is a Single Premium Deferred Annuity.

Subaccount (or Separate Account) - The investment part of a variable deferred annuity. It operates similarly to a mutual fund. The investor owns and controls how the money in this Subaccount is invested. The money in this Subaccount is not commingled with the other money of the life insurance company.

Surrender Charge - Just as with life insurance, there can be a Surrender Charge for surrendering a deferred annuity during the early years of the contract. This Surrender Charge varies from company to company and even from policy to policy. Investigate any Surrender Charge before investing in an annuity.

Variable Deferred Annuity - A Variable Deferred Annuity is considered a securities product and it is therefore required to be sold with a prospectus. The investment monies in a Variable Deferred Annuity are placed in a subaccount or separate account. The investment options available in this subaccount

206

are many. The subaccount operates similarly to a mutual fund. The monies in this subaccount can be invested in stocks, bonds, money market securities or even a combination of all three. The investment earnings grow tax deferred until withdrawn inside a Variable Deferred Annuity.

PART V

Some Other Fundamentals

◆

CHAPTER
◆ 13 ◆

UNDERSTANDING THE ECONOMIC NEWS

ADRIFT IN A SEA OF INFORMATION

Many people feel overwhelmed by the sheer volume of economic news coming at them through television, radio, newspapers and magazines. This is not surprising, since very few have had any economic education in school or their homes. Not only are most of us ill prepared to comprehend the meaning of this economic news, but we also believe it to be highly complex and difficult to understand.

WHY PAY ATTENTION TO THE ECONOMY?

The economy has a powerful impact on the market value of debt and equity investments, both on a day-to-day basis and over the long haul. Investors, mutual fund managers, insurance companies, pension funds, among others, make short and long-term financial decisions, depending on whether the economy or sectors of the economy are expanding, booming, declining or in a recession. It therefore makes sense that you should follow the economic news in order to make intelligent investment choices.

NOT AS OVERWHELMING AS IT LOOKS

You do not need to have a Harvard MBA to make sense of the economic news available in magazines, newspapers and broadcast media. You simply need to become aware of the primary elements that drive our economy. First, read the simple explanations in the following paragraphs. Next, scan the clearly defined terms at the end of the chapter. This material will guide you to a fundamental understanding of forces that both impact and reflect the state of the economy. Finally, for a deeper understanding, pick up the easy-to-read books recommended in this chapter. If you follow these basic steps, you'll soon be charting your own course through an apparent ocean of financial and economic news.

WHAT IS ECONOMICS?

There is no universally accepted definition of economics. Some economists say it is the science of the production, distribution and consumption of goods and services. We'll look primarily at Macroeconomics—which is the study of the big picture of the economy as a whole. Microeconomics—the small picture—is the study of individuals, families, companies and industries.

PREDICTING THE ECONOMY

The economy does not perform in an even and predictable pattern, just as no football game is played in an exactly predictable order. Nonetheless, certain measurable variables, although mathematically inexact, can give us strong indications of how a season is likely to turn out for a football team. Similarly, there are many measurable variables, albeit imprecise, that tell us where the economy is at and where it is headed. They are called economic indicators.

THE MAJOR ECONOMIC INDICATORS

GROSS DOMESTIC PRODUCT

The Gross Domestic Product (GDP) is published quarterly. It tells us about the nation's economic output and spending. The GDP is closely monitored by investors, money managers, Congress, the President, the Federal Reserve Board and economists. An increase or decrease in the GDP in any one quarter, but definitely in any two or three consecutive quarters, clearly signals that the economy is expanding or heading into a recession. This figure is reviewed at length in the financial press. Even if you do not have time to keep up with many of the economic indicators discussed below, never omit tuning in to reports on the GDP. Almost all other indicators supply information about the GDP.

AUTOMOBILE SALES

Automobile sales reports are released every ten days. Since it is released so often, it is a leading indicator of the strength or weakness of the economy. If auto sales decrease, then the economy may be heading into a recession. If, during a recession, you hear that auto sales are rebounding, then the economy is likely on an upward turn and recovering. This is one economic indicator that you probably are already familiar with.

EMPLOYMENT

There are very few people who do not have a basic understanding of this report and what it means. It is a very important barometer of the nation's economic health. It is published quarterly, but revised monthly, because it is often difficult to get accurate figures. If the unemployment rate declines, it is generally perceived as good news. But a very low rate of unemployment can ignite fears of an inflation spiral and cause the Federal Reserve Board to increase short-term interest rates. This can have an important impact on the market value of many investments.

PRODUCER PRICE INDEX (PPI)

The producer price index is published monthly and it is a leading indicator on the rate of inflation. The figures released are examined closely by the Federal Reserve Board. It is difficult for beginners to appreciate the destructive power of a high inflation rate and why so much ink, words and deeds are devoted to managing it. Therefore, read up when you can on the impact of inflation on the investment markets, in people's lives and also find out about the efforts to control it without causing people severe economic hardship.

RETAIL SALES

This report is published monthly by the Commerce Department but it is subject to major revisions. An increase or decrease in retail sales is a sign of which direction the economy is headed. A strong retail sector is good news for stock prices and usually bad news for fixed income investments, such as bonds and money market securities.

HOUSING STARTS AND BUILDING PERMITS

This is an easy and very useful guidepost for most people to understand. Positive changes in housing starts, building permits and automobile sales are the first barometers to signal an economic turnaround from a recession. On the other hand, a decline in housing starts, building permits and auto sales are major indicators of an economic slowdown.

CONSUMER PRICE INDEX (CPI)

The consumer price index is published monthly. It is a measure of inflation. The CPI tells us if consumer prices are going up or down and by how much. If consumer prices are increasing rapidly, say at an annual rate of 4% to 6%, then the Federal Reserve Board will increase short-term interest rates in an attempt to curtail consumer spending and reduce inflation.

PERSONAL INCOME AND CONSUMPTION EXPENDITURES

The U.S. Department of Commerce publishes this report monthly. It is an important and easy economic indicator for the person on the street to follow. Personal consumption expenditures comprise over half of the GDP. So whether personal consumption expenditures are increasing or decreasing tells forecasters what direction the economy is headed. The figures on personal income growth or decline are an important piece of data in signaling the immediate future direction of the economy. A growth in income indicates there is more money available for spending and a decline is a sign of a likely tightening in people's consumer habits.

THE INDEX OF LEADING ECONOMIC INDICATORS

The index of leading economic indicators is a composite of eleven separate indicators. This index is used as a guide in determining when the economy is changing direction. It is published on the last day of the month by the U.S. Department of Commerce. Forecasters usually interpret three consecutive months of the same directional change in the index as an important turning point in the economy either up or down. That is why it is said to be a leading indicator, as it is designed to help forecast future economic activity. It is not important, at least for now, that you commit to memory the eleven indexes that comprise the index of leading economic indicators.

NEW HOME SALES

This economic indicator is also easy to follow. The Department of Commerce publishes this indicator monthly. New home sales are an important economic guide that reflect activity in a key portion of the economy. If new home sales are increasing or strong, then the economy is likely to be robust and sound. But if new home sales are declining or in the doldrums, then the economy is probably headed into a recession or already in a recession. Besides auto sales, it is a key leading indicator of an economic recovery or an economic slowdown.

CONSTRUCTION SPENDING

The Department of Commerce publishes this report monthly. Since it represents a sizable portion of the GDP, it is closely monitored by economists, investors, the Federal Reserve Board and politicians. Like auto and home sales, it is a leading indicator of economic activity. A downturn in construction spending signals a possible downturn in the economy and an increase in construction spending indicates a likely upturn in economic activity. These reports are subject to significant revisions, so one month's report is not usually given much weight. Several months of similar reports, without any obvious reason why there might be an alteration, is a clear signal of the future direction of the economy.

MERCHANDISE TRADE BALANCE

This economic report is published monthly by the Department of Commerce. It is only of value to the Federal Reserve Board, economists, money managers and politicians. It is certainly not likely to be of any use to beginning investors. Since world trade is assuming a greater importance in our lives every year, you should read about this economic indicator later.

INVESTMENT IMPACT OF THESE ECONOMIC INDICATORS

ON EQUITY INVESTMENTS

The current and expected future outlook for corporate profits (earnings) is the most important factor in determining stock prices. If current earnings are good and projected to grow, then stock prices will generally increase. On the other hand, if current profits are weak or predicted to decline, then stock prices will also decrease.

The state of the economy is the most critical factor that decides corporate profits. If the economy is strong, company profits are likely to be very positive. But if the economy is declining or in a recession, then corporate profits, in general, are likely to be weak. Not all sectors of the economy and certainly not all companies follow the same timetable of economic strength or weakness.

Other factors in addition to the general economy affect the profit or loss picture for a company. Corporate management, technological innovation, productivity growth, cost control measures, interest rates, inflation, research and development and consumer demand are some of these factors.

The state of the economy also has a powerful impact on the market value of another important equity investment—residential real estate. When the economy is strong and unemployment is low, residential real estate values increase. You can also count on real estate prices remaining stagnant or even declining, sometimes severely, if the economy is in a prolonged recession.

AND THEIR IMPACT ON DEBT INVESTMENTS

The market value of debt investments do not respond in the same manner as equity investments to the state of the economy. A strong economy is usually very good news for stock and residential real estate prices but generally bad news for bond prices.

In order to understand how the economy influences the market value of bonds and other debt investments, you must be informed on the impact of Federal Reserve Board short-term interest rate changes. If the economy is expanding rapidly and inflation is escalating to an unacceptable level, the Federal Reserve Board will increase short-term interest rates to slow down the economy and reduce inflation. These short-term interest rate increases will cause existing bonds to decrease in market value. The opposite is also true—if the economy is stagnant or in a recession, the "Fed" will reduce short-term interest rates to stimulate the economy. This action by the "Fed" will cause the market value of existing bonds to increase.

For a more detailed and easy-to-read analysis of how these economic indicators and Federal Reserve Board interest rate changes affect the market value of equity and debt investments, read *The Atlas of Economic Indicators* by W. Stansbury Carnes and Stephen Slifer.

SOME IMPORTANT FORCES THAT IMPACT THE ECONOMY

CONGRESS AND THE PRESIDENT

Just as we make plans for our future and try to carry out those plans, our government also strategizes for a healthy economy. It's a great challenge. Although we are not perfect at meeting this challenge, anyone with a knowledge of history knows we are better at it today than even a hundred years ago. How much government interference should there be in controlling the economy? In all democracies throughout the world, this debate is conducted in the political arena. In our country, this debate is conducted mainly between the President and the Republican and Democratic parties. You can track this discussion by closely following the spending and taxation programs of each party. Far too many people pay no attention to this discourse and dismiss it as politics as usual. Do not participate in this kind of negativism.

FEDERAL RESERVE BOARD

In addition to the President and Congress who control the fiscal policy, through taxation and spending policies, there is another part of the Federal Government that plays a critical role in managing how the economy performs. It is the Federal Reserve Board (FRB), and it regulates the money supply and monetary policy of the nation.

The Federal Reserve Board has the power to check the money supply in many ways. When the FRB wants the economy to expand, it decreases short-term interest rates, and when it wants to slow down the economy to reduce inflation, it increases short-term interest rates. Of course it gets more complicated than this. Tune in to the perpetual debate among the President, politicians of both parties, economists, commentators and money managers about what the Federal Reserve Board is doing or should be doing with interest rates. Initially, this discussion may seem dull, compared to the rest of the news. As your investment

218

knowledge grows, however, so also will your interest in the pronouncements of the FRB.

HUMAN EMOTIONS

Human emotions have a powerful affect on the economy and the investment markets in the short-term. Most of us get more optimistic and confident than we ought to during a booming economy and become too pessimistic and fearful during a recession. During a boom, many people spend like there is no tomorrow. Production cannot keep up with consumer demand and so prices start to rise, sometimes rapidly. This sets off an inflation spiral. As you begin to understand the destructive effects a high inflation rate can have on a country, you will appreciate the war of words among economists, politicians, money managers and others who advocate various ways to control inflation without causing undue economic hardship to millions of people.

SUMMARY

The overall state of our national economy has an enormous impact on the market value of investments. In an expanding economy, stocks and residential real estate are likely to increase in market value. When the economy is contracting or weak, stocks and residential real estate usually decrease in value. Of course, not every stock or piece of residential real estate follows this general pattern.

Bonds and other debt investments do not respond in the same manner as stock prices to the ups and downs of the economy. A strong economy is good news for stock prices but usually bad news for existing bond prices. When the economy is very strong, inflation is likely to increase and so the "Fed" hikes short-term interest rates to slow down the economy. This causes existing bond prices to decline. On the other hand, when the economy is weak and in a recession, the "Fed" reduces interest rates. This causes the market price of existing bonds to increase.

The major economic indicators are important guideposts that tell us if the economy is expanding, very strong, contracting or in a recession.

The easiest indicators to follow are the GDP, auto and home sales, retail sales, employment figures and the consumer price index. Data on these economic indicators are published regularly by government departments. They are reported in the press, television, radio and finance magazines. Economists, politicians, money managers, financial commentators, the Federal Reserve Board and individual investors analyze this data.

Congress, the President and the Federal Reserve Board each have major powers that influence the economy. Congress and the President control the fiscal policy—taxation and spending—of the country and the Federal Reserve Board controls the monetary policy. The main power of the FRB is its authority to raise or lower short-term interest rates. These political and economic powers vested in Congress, the President and the FRB can materially impact the market value of investments in both the short and long-term.

Human emotions—fear, greed, irrational exuberance and unwarranted pessimism—can dramatically influence the economy and the market value of investments in the short-term. Rumors and even remarks of supposedly unbiased analysts have precipitated sudden spikes or spirals in a company's stock. The phenomena of the ubiquitous "dot.com" companies, which crashed to earth in early 2000, shows how reason can be swept aside. The economy and investment markets are both rational and efficient over the long haul. In the long-term, irrational human behavior becomes discounted and the fundamental laws of economics and investing prevail.

YOUR ECONOMIC NEWS GAME PLAN

◗ *To anticipate what direction the economy is headed, you should follow the major economic indicators—GDP, auto sales, employment, retail sales, the consumer price index and home sales.* Be aware that the economy has expansion and contraction cycles which materially affect the market value of investments. None of these cycles are the same in length and neither economists or the Federal Reserve Board can accurately predict these cycles

◗ *Pay close attention to the actions of the Federal Reserve Board, Congress and the President because they have a powerful influence on the economy and consequently on the market value of investments.* The FRB has the power to raise or lower short-term interest rates. Congress and the President control government spending and taxation.

◗ *Chart your plan for the long haul and avoid being caught in the whirlwind of market fluctuations that human emotions can generate.* Human emotions—such as fear, greed, unwarranted optimism and undue pessimism—play a significant role in how the economy performs. In the short-term, these emotions can also have a great influence on the stock market, or at least specific segments of the stock market. Over the long-haul, it is the fundamentals—such as corporate profits and company management—that are the main determinants of stock prices.

◗ *Familiarize yourself with the terminology section that follows.* It will be a useful reference to consult as you read the books recommended here. Do not try to remember and understand all of them in one sitting.

◗ *Read the following books, all are written in language accessible to beginners:*

➢ *The Atlas of Economic Indicators* by W. Stansbury Carnes and Stephen Slifer. This book does a superb job of explaining, in layman's language, the major economic indicators, the role of the Federal Reserve Board, and their impact on the market value of various investments.

➤ *From Here to Economy* by Todd Buccholtz. Buccholtz has overcome the "handicap" of having advanced degrees from both Cambridge University and Harvard Law School and has written a most readable, entertaining and even humorous book about the economy. In his introduction Mr. Buccholtz makes the case for both a chapter on the economic news in this book and also for reading his book: "Many people want to learn economics because they want to help themselves perform better as investors."

➤ *A Beginner's Guide to the World Economy* by Randy Epping. Epping explains seventy-one basic economic concepts, such as macroeconomics, international trade, central bank, stock index and inflation. There is an excellent glossary of economic and financial terms.

➤ *How to Read the Financial Pages* by Peter Passell. This small paperback will help you to decipher the financial data in your daily newspaper. For now, concentrate on areas covered in this book.

At the end of this book, you will find a mail order form for these four excellent books.

UNDERSTANDING THE ECONOMIC NEWS— TERMINOLOGY

Adam Smith - Often called the father of modern economics. Adam Smith was an eighteenth century Scotsman who believed that the economic markets should take care of themselves. He maintained that there should be minimal or even no government interference in the marketplace. His book, *The Wealth Of Nations*, is today studied in many universities and financial learning centers throughout the world. It provided the foundation for our present day capitalist system.

Balance of Trade - The difference in amounts of money between what a country exports and imports.

Business Cycle - The pattern of economic expansion and contraction in a country. Governments today are better at controlling runaway economic expansion—thereby preventing inflation. They can also implement measures to head off a severe recession. Human behavior, however, remains very difficult to manage.

Consumer Price Index (CPI) - The average increase or decrease in the price of a certain package of goods. It is published monthly by the Bureau of Labor Statistics and followed closely by investors, the government and the Federal Reserve Board.

Cost-of-Living Adjustment (COLA) - An adjustment either up or down in many government benefit programs, such as Social Security, which are tied to the Cost-of-Living index.

Deficit - The amount that outlays and expenditures exceed receipts and revenues.

Depression - This is when unemployment rises substantially and the economy remains at a standstill and productivity declines considerably. Such conditions were present in the Great Depression of the 1930s. Although some people fear that we could have an economic depression similar to the

30s, most economists feel that the government could swiftly implement measures and legislation, if necessary, to prevent a depression.

Deregulation - The removing of government restrictions on companies and industries. The intent of deregulation is to increase competition and make the economy more productive. Many industries, such as the airlines, trucking, telephones and power companies have been deregulated in the past few decades. The banking, financial services and insurance industries are currently undergoing deregulation. That is why you can see a blurring of the services offered by each of these financial institutions. Insurance companies are now offering financial and some banking services. Banks have added financial and insurance services to their repertoire. Securities companies are selling variable life insurance and variable annuities.

Discount Rate - The amount charged by the Federal Reserve Bank to its member banks to borrow money.

Disposable Income - The amount of personal income left after taxes and other deductions from gross income.

Dumping - This term describes the sale of goods at a price below their actual cost. Both companies and countries have perpetrated this practice with the intention of gaining a monopoly by driving competitors out of the marketplace. They then raise prices and make exorbitant profits.

Easy Credit - An economic period in which banks and other financial institutions reject few applicants for loans. This is in contrast to a tight credit market in which many applicants are turned down for loans.

Economic Indicators - These economic data sources tell investors, politicians, the Federal Reserve Board and the public where the economy is at and seems to be headed. Every day the major news media report these Economic Indicators, such as housing starts, auto sales and the unemployment rate. Try to become familiar with several of them. They will help give you some idea whether the economy is in an expansion or contraction cycle. For example, if auto and home sales are declining, then home prices are likely to decline and interest rates will probably decrease.

Federal Funds - The rate at which member banks of the Federal Reserve Bank lend each other money. These loans are for very short periods, such as overnight.

Federal Reserve Board - Congress created the Federal Reserve Bank System in 1913. The Federal Reserve controls the nation's money supply through its many powers. Think of the Federal Reserve as the central bank that all other banks feed from. The banking system is headed by a seven member Board of Governors, who are appointed by the President and confirmed by the Senate. The Federal Reserve Board Chairman is the most important person on this board and in our banking system. Neither beginning or experienced investor need know all the details about how the Federal Reserve System works. You should certainly be aware of the power of the Federal Reserve Board—popularly known as "The Fed"—to lower or raise short-term interest rates.

Fiscal Policy - The U.S. Government in Washington D.C., controls the Fiscal Policy of the country through its taxation and spending policies. The government can increase or reduce various taxes and it can also increase or reduce government spending in order to achieve certain economic goals.

Gross Domestic Product (GDP) - The output of final goods and services in the country as measured in dollars and cents in a one year period. Journalists regularly report and speculate on the expansion and contraction of the GDP. You should become very familiar with this important economic indicator and follow it regularly in the media. If, for example, the

GDP is growing at a moderate pace, then stock prices in general are likely to increase. If the GDP is stagnant or declining, which it does during a recession, then stock prices, in general, are likely to decline.

Growth Rate - The percentage Growth Rate of the GDP. Since the GDP is discussed and written about so much in the electronic and print media, you are also going to hear and see a lot about the economy's percentage Growth Rate from year to year and even quarter to quarter. During a recession, we may have a negative Growth Rate. In other words, the economic output of the country may be a percentage point or two less than the previous year. The GDP Growth Rate is always measured by some prior period, such as a quarter, a year, ten years or some other longer period. Also analysts compare our GDP Growth Rate to other countries. A very high Growth Rate is not always good news for a country because it could trigger an inflation spiral.

Index of Leading Economic Indicators - A group of economic indicators that give us a good idea about future economic prospects. There are eleven indicators that comprise the Index of Leading Economic Indicators. They are sometimes called the "Composite Index of 11 Leading Economic Indicators." The Index of Leading Economic Indicators tell us whether the economy is expanding, and if so, in what areas. These Indicators also tell us whether the economy is declining or heading into a recession. Investors, economists, politicians and the Federal Reserve Board follow this data closely.

Inflation - An increase in the price of goods and services. Annual increases of anywhere between 1% and 3% in the price of goods and services seems to be acceptable in capitalist countries. Any increase in the price of goods and services beyond 3% to 4% annually causes economists, politicians and the Federal Reserve Board grave concern.

Inflation Rate - The percentage rate at which prices and services increases from quarter to quarter, year to year or some other time period.

Inflation Spiral - A period of time characterized by a rapid increase in the price of goods and services. During the late 1970s and early 1980s we had such an Inflation Spiral. In order to bring this Inflation Spiral under control, the Federal Reserve Board increased short-term interest rates beyond what they had been since the Federal Reserve was established in 1913.

Institutional Investors - Institutional Investors are known as the "big guns" of the investment world. Examples of Institutional Investors are insurance companies, pension funds, mutual funds and banks. It is difficult to imagine the huge sums of money these Institutional Investors can move about, even from country to country, in just seconds. These billions of dollars, yens, pounds or deutchmarks, can be transferred globally with the flick of a computer button. We are now in a global investment, economic and financial world.

Interest - The amount of money charged by a lender for borrowing money. It is usually expressed as an annual percentage rate, like 6%, 8%, or 10%.

Keynesian Economics - John Keynes, a British economist, espoused an economic theory asserting that governments should use their tax and spending powers to end recessions. According to Keynesian (pronounced Kanezian) economics, this can be accomplished by reducing taxes and increasing government programs. Conversely, governments can avert a higher inflation rate if they increase taxes and reduce spending during economic booms. Keynesian Economics is accepted today as being a far more enlightened economic theory than Laissez-Faire Economics. Democrats in this country embrace Keynesian Economics more than Republicans, but it is only a matter of degree. President Nixon, a Republican, once proclaimed that "we are all Keynesians now."

Lagging Economic Indicators - Economic Indicators that reach their crest after a peak in economic expansion and a trough after the economy has hit bottom in the economic cycle. These indicators, since they are said to be Lagging Economic Indicators, are not monitored as much as the index of leading economic indicators.

Laissez-Faire - This French term literally means "to let do," to let people do as they please. In the economic sense, the Laissez-Faire doctrine opposed government interference in the economy. Adam Smith, author of *The Wealth of Nations*, advocated this kind of government policy which was practiced more in the nineteenth century than in the twentieth. Keynesian economics has been more espoused in capitalist countries since the Great Depression of the 1930s than Laissez-Faire economic theory. The debate today between our major political parties is over the degree and circumstances of government intervention.

Macroeconomics - Often referred to as the "big picture," in contrast to Microeconomics, which is referred to as the "small picture." Macroeconomics is the study of the economy as a whole, taking into consideration such factors as unemployment, inflation, growth rate and government spending. Microeconomics is the study of small units in the economy, such as individuals, companies and households. You only need to be generally aware of these terms. You will hear them used often and in many contexts.

Monetary Policy - The Federal Reserve Board controls the Monetary Policy of the country, primarily through the money supply and interest rates. You will repeatedly see news coverage of any plans the Federal Reserve Board may have for raising or lowering interest rates. What the FRB, commonly called "The Fed," is doing or should be doing with interest rates remains a constant debate among politicians, economists and investors. You should follow this discussion.

Prime Rate - This is the interest rate banks charge their most creditworthy customers. It is directly affected by what the Federal Reserve Board charges its member banks to borrow from the Federal Reserve Bank. If you look at a graph of the Prime Rate and the Federal Funds Rate, you'll see them move in tandem with interest rate changes by the Federal Reserve Board.

Recession - A severe economic downturn, though nowhere as severe as a depression. Most Recessions have lasted about a year. A decline in some of the economic indicators that comprise the index of leading economic indicators are the first signs of a recession. For example, a downturn in retail sales for two quarters in a row will certainly cause economists to wonder if a Recession is not only on its way but in full force. Sometimes this is not clear until more economic data is available.

Unemployment - A word that should mean the same for everybody or so it would seem. Most of us think it means those not working in the labor force who do want to work, but it gets more complicated than that. Most economists take full employment to mean a rate of unemployment below 5 %. If the unemployment rate is below 5 % or thereabouts, then an unacceptable inflation level becomes more likely. A very low unemployment rate, say 3 %, will cause a demand for higher wages and then we are likely to see higher prices and maybe an inflation spiral. The ways governments can reduce unemployment to its absolute minimum while keeping inflation under control causes regular debate and many new economic theories from financial learning centers.

Wage Spiral - A period in which wages are rising rapidly. It is a period with low unemployment. The government usually decides to intervene in some way to control any wage spiral. It is normally done by the Federal Reserve Board raising short-term interest rates.

CHAPTER
◆ 14 ◆

YOUR CHILD'S COLLEGE INVESTMENT PLAN

A Fun Game Plan

I f you trust in the maxim "two heads are better than one" when confronting certain challenges, then putting together your child's college investment plan could be one of the most rewarding opportunities you will have to practice this principle. How do you start getting two heads working together on this challenge?

STOCK MARKET GAME

First, call the Securities Industry Association (SIA) at 212-618-0519 and order the *Stock Market Game*. It may take a few weeks for it to arrive. The Stock Market Game is a ten-week program designed and promoted by the Securities Industry Association (SIA) for students in grades 4-12. It introduces them to the world of stock market investing, economics and business. Although the mathematical computations are not complicated in the Stock Market Game, some mathematics teachers find it useful to show the students the practical application of their academic work in the "real-world."

WHY THE *STOCK MARKET GAME?*

Many parents invest for their child's college education through traditional savings plans and fixed life insurance. The purchasing power of this money grows very little, if at all, with these investments. Sometimes it even declines because of taxes on investment earnings and inflation. Consequently, they may not have an adequate investment amount accumulated for their child to attend the university of his or her choice.

Very likely many parents know that they should be investing in stocks for greater long-term growth, but assume that stock market investing is difficult to understand and "risky." They probably are aware that investing in stocks provides better returns over an extended period of time than traditional savings plans or fixed life insurance.

The *Stock Market Game* can be a wonderful vehicle to help your child understand the fundamentals of stock market investing. If your child is enjoying learning about stocks and reading several books on stock market investing, you certainly could have a great partner in planning his or her college investment plan.

DON'T GIVE IN TO THE TEMPTATION

You may be tempted to give the Securities Industry Association (SIA) phone number to one of your child's teachers and let the teacher take it from there. Do not do this. Most teachers have never heard of the *Stock Market Game.* They may be reluctant, if left to their own devices, to spend time learning about this investment educational tool.

Read the instructions about how the game is set up and played. Then select one of your child's teachers, preferably in the business, economics or personal finance departments (if such departments exist) or his or her mathematics teacher. There is some work involved in setting up the game. Offer to help. Of course, all the other students will benefit from your efforts. Consider it part of your contribution to a better society. Besides, your child is likely to be very proud of your support and also very helpful.

You may get some press coverage, especially if you or the teacher know a little about public relations. The local press is usually eager to publicize something positive and interesting that is going on in schools. There is some small cost involved in setting up the game. Many businesses will be glad to underwrite these costs, especially if they can get publicity out of such an arrangement. You could name each team (four players to a team) after their business sponsors. Make sure your child and possibly some other children in the class assist in this endeavor. Don't be surprised if your child takes over the leadership role.

SOME MORE GREAT READING

While your child is playing the ten-week Stock Market Game, have him or her read *The Totally Awesome Money Book for Kids and Their Parents* by Adriane Berg and her son Arthur Berg Bochner. This book is written in a style that most students will easily understand. If your child absorbs the information in this book like a sponge, then present him or her with the book *One Up On Wall Street* by Peter Lynch with John Rothchild.

After participating in this ten-week session of the Stock Market Game and reading *The Totally Awesome Money Book For Kids and Their Parents* and *One Up On Wall Street,* you and your child may decide to go the route of purchasing individual stocks. If you do opt for investing in individual stocks, you should join a local investment club. You can locate an investment club in your area by contacting the National Association of Investors Corporation (NAIC) at 248-583-6242.

The *Stock Market Game* will take some work on your part, but your child's response may be more than ample reward for your efforts. You will not only be rewarded emotionally and financially, but you will also be showing your child how to invest for a lifetime.

YOUR CHILD'S COLLEGE INVESTMENT GAME PLAN

● *Call the Securities Industry Association at 212-618-0519 and order their Stock Market Game.* When you receive the package, read the instructions. Become familiar with the rules of how the game is set up and played. Show it to one of your child's teachers, preferably in the business or mathematics department, and offer to help getting it started.

● *Have your child read* The Totally Awesome Money Book For Kids And Their Parents *by Adriane Berg and her son Arthur Berg Bochner, during the ten weeks of the Stock Market Game.* Presuming your child shows a keen interest in playing the Stock Market Game, then present him or her with the book One Up On Wall Street by Peter Lynch with John Rothchild.

● *If your child appears eager to learn more about stocks after playing the Stock Market Game, find out if there is an investment club for students in your area.* Your child may want to take the leadership position in setting one up at his or her school if you can't find an established club in your area.

To order any of the books I've recommended, see the information at the end of *Quarterback Your Investment Plan.*

CHAPTER
◆ 15 ◆

INVESTMENT ADVISORS

Who Should You Consult?

There are very few angels in the financial services. Neither are there many devils. Yet most people today tend to vilify all sales people and representatives because of the major sins of the few.

There probably has never been an era in the history of this country like the past quarter century where so many jump to blame others for what they believe are society's ills. This phenomenon of faulting others is not only prevalent in the financial services arena, but also in the political, educational, medical and legal fields. It seems to me that most of us are long overdue to take a good look in the mirror and examine our contribution to this "sickness."

I do not deny that victims and perpetrators exist in society. I contend, however, that our schools fail to arm us with the knowledge that could protect us from joining the ranks of the victim. It, therefore, falls on us to educate ourselves about this crucial area of our lives.

There remains much room for improvement in the ethical practices of the financial services industry. Even more importantly, there remains a great unmet need in our schools to dramatically increase the teaching of personal finance. Only by such teaching can we prepare our children to make intelligent future financial choices. For example, if students were better informed about credit card debt and personal finance in high school, do you think so many college students and recent college graduates would fall prey to the easy, uncollateralized, high-interest loans pushed by credit card companies?

SALESPEOPLE ARE WAY OVERRATED

Most of us tend to believe the stereotype of financial companies and their representatives as great scheming sales strategists. In doing so, we overestimate their cunning, thereby giving them an unjustified psychological advantage over our decisions. They usually only seem so shrewd and manipulative because most consumers are uninformed about the basics of the financial product being considered for purchase.

As a result of inadequate schooling in the fundamentals of personal finance, you may now feel that you face the problem of playing catch-up in a hurry. This book can help you confront and conquer a major portion of this challenge over the next several months. Regard this book as your personal investment coach. Simply follow the instructions for learning the fundamentals of investing, including the terminology and the characteristics of the major investment players discussed in this book—stocks, bonds, money market securities, savings accounts, mutual funds and residential real estate.

Once you have done this, you are ready to gain a deeper understanding of these players by reading the carefully selected books recommended at the end of most chapters. Having done this, I'm sure you will be able to decide easily what additional investment advisors, if indeed any, you should consult in your quest to become a star quarterback of your investment plan.

YOUR INVESTMENT ADVISOR'S GAME PLAN

Become knowledgeable on the fundamentals of investing before consulting any financial planner or financial services representative. This is easier than you may now believe. Read more about the major investment players, especially stocks, bonds and mutual funds. You simply cannot get any better than Peter Lynch in *One Up On Wall Street,* Annette Thau in *The Bond Book* and John Bogle in *Bogle on Mutual Funds.* Before you read all three, make sure you have a solid grounding in the fundamentals discussed throughout this book.

Next, you should listen and watch a great investment advisor and his guests on public television. Tune in on Friday evenings and watch "Wall Street Week" with Louis Rukeyser. Keep in mind when watching this program, or indeed any television program about investing, that there probably will be an overemphasis and overanalysis on issues current at the time of taping, rather than focusing on the long-term outlook of various investment players.

INVESTMENT ADVISORS—TERMINOLOGY

Account Executive - A stockbroker. Sometimes they are called registered representatives. An Account Executive must pass an exam administered by the NASD (National Association of Securities Dealers) in order to sell securities, such as stocks, bonds, money market securities and mutual funds.

Back-End Load - Often called a contingent deferred sales charge (CDSC). It is a fee charged for redeeming securities before a certain period of time. A Back-End Load is charged in lieu of a Front-End Load. Usually this Back-End Load is on a sliding scale and ends after several years.

Brokerage Fee - A fee charged by a brokerage firm for transacting sales and providing services to investors. Merrill Lynch, Paine Weber, A.G. Edwards and many others are called full service brokerage companies. Charles Schwab and Quick and Reilly are called discount brokerages. There are now some brokerage firms that are known as deep discounters. Knowledgeable investors usually use the services of discount brokerages and deep discounters.

Certified Financial Planner (CFP) - A person who has completed a series of rigorous financial planning correspondence courses and passed a ten hour examination. Many colleges and universities offer courses that help qualify a person to be a CFP. The CFP degree is conferred by the Institute of Certified Financial Planners in Denver, Colorado.

Certified Life Underwriter (CLU) - A finance degree whose major emphasis is life insurance. It is conferred by the American College in Bryan Mawr, Pennsylvania, on life insurance agents.

Chartered Financial Consultant (ChFC) - A finance degree, similar to the CFP degree, that is conferred on individuals by the American College in Bryan Mawr, Pennsylvania.

Churning - A financial services representative's unethical conduct that encourages people to trade securities and life insurance policies for no other purpose than to generate commissions.

Fee-Based Financial Planner - A financial planner who charges a fee for his or her investment and financial planning services. Usually, she will place a client's investments and insurance with no-load companies. Only a small percentage of financial planners are Fee-Based Financial Planners.

Financial Planner - A person who evaluates and helps individuals accomplish their financial needs and goals. Financial planning encompasses several areas of finance, particularly investments, insurance and income taxes. Many people who call themselves financial planners do not know about all the major areas of personal finance and do not offer advice or services in all these areas. Your best protection against incompetent planners is knowing the basics of personal finance.

Front-End Load - A sales commission or charge to purchase securities or other financial products. Many securities and other financial products are now sold by no-load companies. Knowledgeable investors usually use the services of no-load companies.

Load - A sales commission or service charge for buying securities or other financial products.

Load Mutual Fund - A Mutual Fund that charges a commission for buying shares in the fund.

Stockbroker - Sometimes called a registered representative or account executive or investment advisor. They buy and sell securities on behalf of investors and also offer advise and provide information in order for their clients to make intelligent investment decisions. They can be financially compensated in several ways. The usual method is a percentage sales charge of the amount invested.

CHAPTER
♦ 16 ♦

THE EIGHTH
WONDER
OF THE WORLD
RE-EXAMINED

IT WILL NOT TAKE LONG

Baron Rothchild once said he did not know what the seven wonders of the world were, but that he knew what the eighth was—compound interest. Throughout history, the prolific way money grows—through the principle of compounding—has fascinated men of great ideas—from Benjamin Franklin to Albert Einstein. If such giants of the world of money and ideas have said that compound interest is such a marvel, should we not just forego this re-examination? Well, this review will not take long, and it may indeed be well worth a few moments of your time.

WHAT IS COMPOUND INTEREST?

Simple interest means paying interest on the principal only. Compound interest is the paying of interest on both the principal and any interest already earned. Savings and loans and banks pay compound interest on savings accounts and certificates of deposit. This compounding of interest may be done daily, weekly, monthly, quarterly, yearly or at some other interval.

Daily compounding of interest yields more than yearly compounding. For example, a $10,000 certificate of deposit that pays simple interest, at a rate of 10% annually, will earn $1,000 interest each year. On the other hand, if that same $10,000 were earning 10% compounded semiannually, the interest gained would be $1,025 after one year. If it were earning 10% compounded quarterly, it would yield $1,038.13. If it were compounded monthly, the interest would be $1,047.13, and compounded daily, it would be $1,061.56.

INVESTMENT RETURNS USING THIS PRINCIPLE

FOR SOME—DISAPOINTING AND ALSO TRAGIC

Millions of people have used the principle of the compounding of investment returns faithfully throughout their lives and certainly have yet to see the eighth wonder of the world as a consequence. In fact, the results were often disappointing and in many instances tragic. Why so? Their compounded returns were not sufficient to offset the terrible twins—taxes and inflation—and so the purchasing power of their invested monies declined over time. Many of these people needed the purchasing power of most of their invested dollars to increase significantly in order to live the lifestyle they had hoped and dreamed they would have during their retirement years.

FOR OTHERS—EYEPOPPING

Millions of others during this same time period have used the principle of the compounding of investment returns and have, like Baron Rothchild, believed they have seen the eighth wonder of the world.

WHY SUCH DIFFERENT OUTCOMES?

The critical difference was the average rate at which the compounding of investment returns occurred for each group.

Take a close look at the following returns of $1,000 invested annually for twenty-five years earning a compounded return of 4% and also at 10%. The total return after twenty-five years, at 4% compounded annually, is $43,300, and earning 10%, it is $108,200. Take a look at another example. An initial investment of $25,000, with no subsequent additions, earning 4% compounded annually, will return $66,600 after twenty-five years. That same investment amount, at a rate of 10% compounded annually, will return $270,900 after twenty-five years.

HISTORIC RATES OF INVESTMENT RETURNS

These two rates of compounded returns—4% and 10%—have been selected for a specific reason. Since 1925, the investment players that usually appear in the bottom tier of the typical pyramid graph showing levels of investment risk include: passbook savings accounts, certificates of deposit, money market securities, fixed life insurance, fixed annuities, U.S. Treasury bills and other investments have yielded, as a group, about a 4% average annual return. During that same time period, which includes the Great Depression, U.S. common stocks have yielded an annual average return of just over 10%. By the way, the annual average return on U.S. common stocks has been higher than 10% during the past quarter century. Meanwhile, the 4% annual average return achieved by millions of people was usually insufficient to offset the rate of inflation and taxation of investment gains combined.

ACHIEVING SATISFACTORY INVESTMENT RETURNS

How difficult would it have been for the group who achieved about a 4 % return to achieve a 10 %, or more growth in their invested dollars during their earning years? According to Dr. Benjamin Graham, in his 1949 investment classic *The Intelligent Investor*:

> To achieve satisfactory investment results is easier than most people realize.

What was true then is even more true today. Since 1949, a revolutionary new method of investing, particularly in common stocks, has taken a dominant position in the market. This method, "index investing," was pioneered by others but brought to the forefront by The Vanguard Group, under its founder, John Bogle. It has opened the door for beginning and experienced investors alike to achieve satisfactory investment results with minimal effort. This relatively new method of investing, especially in common stocks, has skyrocketed in popularity during the past two decades. Its popularity is now also increasing in the bond market. Combine this new method of investing in common stocks with another relatively new method of investing—"dollar-cost-averaging"—and you have a powerful, yet very simple formula for achieving satisfactory investment returns.

ACHIEVING SUPERIOR INVESTMENT RESULTS

If you want to take up the challenge later of achieving greater investment yardage gains than through index investing, you would do well to heed Dr. Benjamin Graham's observation:

> *To achieve superior results is harder than it looks.*

In his introduction to the fourth revised edition of *The Intelligent Investor* published in 1973, Dr. Graham states what should be a great source of inspiration but also an important warning to you as a beginning investor:

The art of investment has one characteristic that is not generally appreciated. A credible, if unspectacular, result can be achieved by the lay investor with a minimum of effort and capability; but to improve this easily attainable standard requires much application and more than a trace of wisdom. If you merely try to bring just a little extra knowledge and cleverness to bear upon your investment program, instead of realizing a little better than normal results, you may well find that you have done worse.

Since anyone—by just buying and holding a representative list—can equal the performance of the market averages, it would seem a comparatively simple matter to "beat the averages"; but as a matter of fact the proportion of smart people who try this and fail is surprisingly large. Even the majority of investment funds, with all their experienced personnel, have not performed so well over the years as have the general market. Allied to the foregoing is the record of the published stock-market predictions of the brokerage houses, for there is strong evidence that their calculated forecasts have been somewhat less reliable than the simple tossing of a coin.

WHY SOME PEOPLE BECOME WEALTHY

There are various reasons why people become wealthy. One reason is that some who are wealthy have inherited it. But there are three reasons why some people become wealthy that are relevant to you as a beginning investor. The first is this: they have invested in ownership type players, such as stocks, real estate and mutual funds.

As a beginning investor, it is very easy and even inexpensive to invest in one important ownership type player—common stocks. You can do so through investing in a stock mutual fund, by dollar-cost-averaging and preferably in a tax sheltered account, such as a 401K, 403B and IRA, if you qualify.

The second reason why many become wealthy is their willingness to invest through ownership players for the long-term. They know that there can be periods of time when ownership players, such as common stocks and real estate, can decrease in market value. But they are also aware of the historical record of the long-term investor being amply rewarded.

The third reason some become rich is their patience and willingness to tolerate market fluctuations and even its occasional volatility. They know that despite wars, recessions, communism and numerous other challenges, the free enterprise capitalist system has grown enormously and financially rewarded people very well throughout the world for the past two hundred years.

Take a very close look in the Appendix section of this book at the historical rates of returns of some of the major investment players reviewed so far—stocks, bonds and U.S. Treasury bills. These figures are provided by Ibbotson Associates in Chicago. Ibbotson Associates is one of the recognized leaders in investment data gathering in this country. Other data experts you will see referenced in financial books, magazines and newspapers are Morningstar and Lipper Analytical Services. This information gives you a great picture of the past, and it enables you to intelligently and confidently plan your financial future.

IN CONCLUSION

One day, because of your intelligent investment planning, you may be able to proclaim compound interest the eighth wonder of the world. In order to do so, you will probably need investment returns that at least exceed the inflation and taxation of investment earnings rate by 3% to 6% annually and over a long period of time. To achieve this goal, you will likely need to invest in common stocks or some other ownership type investment player. The historical evidence supports that you cannot achieve this goal consistently by using investment players that appear in the bottom tier of the graph that typically represents the investment risk of each investment. These bottom tier investments are said by most financial writers and commentators to be either "low risk" or "virtually risk free." Before you accept or act on their theories, you should take a time out—indeed a long time out—and think through what they mean by "low risk" or "virtually risk free." Commentators and financial writers often toss about the term "risk" without regard for the relative risk to an individual investor in light of his or her specific personal and financial circumstances.

PART VI

Your Investment

Game Plan

◆

CHAPTER
◆ 17 ◆

YOUR INVESTMENT GAME PLAN

Many things which cannot be overcome when they are together, yield themselves up when taken little by little.
— *Plutarch, Roman playwright*

In the quest to be a super quarterback of your investment plan, try to avoid comparing yourself to others. Do not become frustrated with where you are now investment-wise and where you believe you should be at this stage of your life. This challenge is, of course, much easier said than done. Many times you may have found yourself overwhelmed, confused and possibly angry at your lack of competence and confidence in investing. You may have even been envious of co-workers or friends who appear to be very knowledgeable in this important area of their lives.

YOUR INVESTMENT GAME PLAN

You can learn the fundamentals about investing and become very confident in your decision-making ability in a very short period of time if you perform the following strategies. Strategy #1 is critical. Many of the other strategies are very easy to perform once you have accomplished this strategy.

Strategy #1:

🏈 *Learn the basics about investing and the fundamentals of the investment players discussed in my book—stocks, bonds, money market securities, mutual funds, savings accounts and residential real estate.*

Strategy #2:

🏈 *Become familiar with the investment and financial terminology at the end of most chapters. Do not try to grasp it all in one reading.*

Strategy #3:

🏈 *Get a clear understanding of the current concept of investment risk, as either written or subscribed to by virtually all investment writers and commentators and also my new and revolutionary concept.* Read Chapter 3 *"Investment Risk—a New and Revolutionary Concept,"* several times. Unless you do, you will likely find yourself starting to gravitate towards the currently accepted concept of investment risk set forth in most books, newspapers, magazines and news analyses.

Strategy #4:

🏈 *Read up on the economic forces that cause the major investment players to fluctuate in market value over the short and long-term.*

Strategy #5:

🏈 *Get a clear picture in your mind of the historic rates of return of the major investment players.* There is an appendix section at the end of my book that provides a graph of the historic investment returns of stocks, bonds, U.S. Treasury bills and also the inflation rate since 1925. It is provided by Ibbotson Associates in Chicago.

Strategy #6:

♦ *Assess your personal and financial circumstances in order to set realistic investment goals.*

Strategy #7:

♦ *Begin investing through mutual funds.* Mutual funds offer today's beginning investor an opportunity to enter the world of investing with great confidence and with few dollars. Many mutual funds will accept as little as $1,000 to buy shares in the fund, and even less if invested in a tax qualified investment plan—such as a 401K, 403B, IRA, Roth IRA, KEOGH or SEP-IRA. There are an endless variety of mutual funds that you can invest through. Many mutual fund families— such as Fidelity, Vanguard and Dreyfus—offer over forty funds that you can invest in. Mutual funds offer diversification, professional management, liquidity and convenience.

Strategy #8:

♦ *Invest in mutual funds through a strategy that has increased dramatically in popularity in the past two decades—index investing.* Not only does index investing make the challenge of deciding which fund or funds to invest in easy, but it may prove to be your investment strategy of choice for many years to come. Both John Bogle in *Bogle on Mutual Funds* and Walter Good and Roy Hermansen in *Index Your Way To Investment Success* make a compelling case for this type of investment strategy. First, read Chapter 9 in *Bogle On Mutual Funds* titled "Index Funds."

If later you want to become a more active investor, then you should become a member of a local investment club. Call and join the National Association of Investors Corporation at (248) 583-6242. The cost to join the NAIC is minimal.

253

Strategy #9:

◆ *Begin and continue investing through a strategy called "Dollar-Cost-Averaging."* This is a strategy whereby you invest the same amount of money at regular intervals, usually monthly, in a mutual fund or other investment. Through dollar-cost-averaging, you get into the habit of regularly investing, regardless of market conditions. You also avoid the challenge of trying to time the market. Given the fact that the biggest stock market gains and losses are concentrated in short periods of time, you avoid the temptation of trying to time the stock market correctly.

Strategy #10:

◆ *Become knowledgeable on the costs of investing.* You can achieve satisfactory to superior investment returns with minimal costs. Read Chapter 10 in *Bogle On Mutual Funds* titled "Mutual Fund Costs" for a comprehensive analysis of the costs associated with investing in mutual funds.

Strategy #11:

◆ *Read more extensively about the major investment players and the economy, once you have mastered the basics in my book.* I recommend that you use the following sequence:

A. *Understanding Wall Street* by Jeffrey Little and Lucien Rhodes. Do not expect to understand every page. For example, it reviews stock options. You can be a great investor without ever knowing what stock options are. Just focus on expanding on what you have learned in this book.

B. *One Up On Wall Street* by Peter Lynch with John Rothchild. This book is recommended at this stage for two specific reasons. One—it is an easy-to-read book on how one of the greatest stockpickers went about the challenge of selecting stocks to buy for the Fidelity Magellan mutual fund, which he managed from 1977 to May 1990. Second—it is

the most inspirational book that I've read so far on investing. Hopefully, you too will find it equally as inspiring.
You will likely need this inspiration in order to create that
intense desire within yourself to be a star quarterback of
your investment plan.

C. *Bogle On Mutual Funds* by John Bogle. Make this book your
investment bible for now and years to come. Bogle clearly
shows that gaining satisfactory investment yardage is
easier than most people think. He also proves that mini-
mizing investment costs and focusing on tax efficiency
are vitally important in achieving excellent investment results.

D. *The Bond Book* by Annette Thau. There may be times that
you feel overwhelmed by all the information. If so, take a
time out and come back later. Reading about debt investments, such as bonds, is not as exciting or interesting as
equity investments. Nonetheless, it is important that you
become knowledgeable about bonds and other debt investment players.

E. *Getting Started in Tax-Savvy Investing* by Andrew
Westhem and Don Korn. Using legitimate tax shelters can
be a powerful tool to supercharge many investment plans.

F. *The Atlas Of Economic Indicators* by W. Stansbury Carnes
and Stephen Slifer. Since it is important to have a basic
understanding of the economy, because it has such a deci-
sive impact on the market value of various investments,
you should make an effort to read about this area sooner
rather than later. *The Atlas Of Economic Indicators* is a
superb, easy-to-read book, to "get your feet wet."

The other books recommended throughout the chapters of my book
may be read in any sequence you choose. At this juncture, you should try
not to be overwhelmed or confused by the information. That's not to say
that you will clearly understand it all. An encyclopedic knowledge of in-

vesting is not necessary. In fact, it can be counterproductive.

Welcome to the world of investing and to the many challenges and opportunities it offers. Always remember, especially now, as you are learning the basics about investing and the major investment players, that gaining satisfactory investment yardage is much easier than most people think.

May you live as long as you want and never want as long as you live. (old Irish proverb)

Your Investment Coach,
Eamonn "Ed" Nohilly

APPENDIX 1

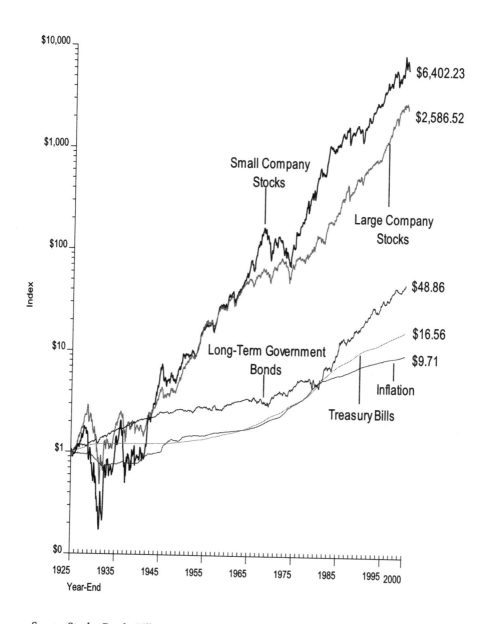

Source: Stocks, Bonds, Bills and Inflation® 2002 Yearbook, ©2002 Ibbotson Associates, Inc.
Based on copyrighted works by Ibbotson and Sinquefield.
All rights reserved. Used with permission.

257

APPENDIX 2

MAJOR MUTUAL FUND COMPANIES

The Vanguard Group 800-662-7447

Fidelity Investments 800-544-8888

Janus 800-525-8983

T. Rowe Price 800-638-5660

Dreyfus 800-373-9387

Neuberger Berman 800-877-9700

Oakmark 800-625-6275

Schwab 800-435-4000

Strong 800-368-1030

Tiaa-Cref 800-842-1924

BIBLIOGRAPHY

Baldwin, Ben. *The New Life Insurance Investment Advisor*. Irwin Publishing, 1994.

Berg, Adrienne and Arthur Berg Bochner. *The Totally Awesome Money Book For Kids And Their Parents*. Newmarket Press, 1993.

Bogle, John. *Bogle On Mutual Funds*. Dell Publishing, 1994.

Breuel, Brian. *The Complete Idiot's Guide To Buying Insurance And Annuities*. Alpha Books, 1996.

Buccholtz, Tod. *From Here To Economy*. Penguin Group, 1995.

Carnes, W. Stansbury and Stephen Slifer. *The Atlas Of Economic Indicators*. Harper Business, 1991.

Carlson, Charles. *Buying Stocks Without A Broker*. McGraw-Hill, 1992.

Crowe, Robert. Editor, *Fundamentals Of Financial Planning*. The American College, Bryan Mawr, PA. 1990.

Eldred, Dr. Gary. *The 106 Common Mistakes Homebuyers Make*. John Wiley, 1994.

Epping, Randy. *A Beginner's Guide To The World Economy*. Vintage Books, 1992.

Farrell, Mary. *Beyond The Basics*. Simon and Schuster, 2000.

Glink, Ilse. *100 Questions Every First Time Home Buyer Should Ask*. Times Books, 1994.

Good, Walter and Roy Hermansen. *Index Your Way To Investment Success*. Printice Hall, 1998.

Graham, Dr. Benjamin. *The Intelligent Investor*. Harper & Row, 1973.

Gross, Bill. *Bill Gross On Investing*. John Wiley, 1997.

Heady, Christy. *The Complete Idiot's Guide To Making Money On Wall Street*. Alpha Books, 1994.

Hecht, Henry and Louis Engel. *How To Buy Stocks*. Bantam Books, 1953.

Ibbotson Associates. *Stocks, Bonds, Bills, And Inflation 2001 Yearbook*. Ibbotson Associates.

Little, Jeffrey and Lucien Rhodes. *Understanding Wall Street*. McGraw-Hill, 1991.

Lynch, Peter with John Rothchild. *One Up On Wall Street*. Penguin, 1989.

Mamis, Justin. *The Nature Of Risk*. Addison-Wesley, 1991.

O'Hara, Thomas and Kenneth Janke, Sr. *Starting and Running a Profitable Investment Club*. Three Rivers Press, 1998.

O'Neill, William J. *How To Make Money In Stocks*. McGraw-Hill, 1988.

Passell, Peter. *How To Read The Financial Pages*. Warner Books, 1986.

Quinn, Jane Bryant. *How To Make The Most Of Your Money*. Simon and Schuster, 1991.

Savage, Terry. *Terry Savage's New Money Strategies For The 90's*. Harper Business, 1993.

Schwab, Charles. *Guide To Financial Independence*. Crown, 1998.

Shapiro, Dr. Alan. *Modern Corporate Finance*. MacMillan, 1990.

Sivy, Michael. *Rules Of Investing – How To Pick Stocks Like A Pro*. Harper business, 1993.

Steinberg, Michael. *Guide To Investing*. New York Institute of Finance, 2000.

Thau, Annette. *The Bond Book*. McGraw-Hill, 1992.

The New York Institute Of Finance. *Stocks Bonds Options Futures*. Prentice-Hall, 1987.

Train, John. *The New Money Masters*. Harper Business, 1989.

VanCaspel, Venita. *Money Dynamics For The 80's*. Reston, 1980.

Westhem, Andrew and Don Korn. *Getting Started In Tax-Savvy Investing*. John Wiley, 2000.

Williamson, Gordon. *Getting Started In Annuities*. John Wiley, 1998.

INDEX

BOOK LIST

INVESTING IN GENERAL

Book # 1   *Quarterback Your Investment Plan—*
The Basics For Beginners .... $ 19.95
By Eamonn "Ed" Nohilly

Book # 2   *Understanding Wall Street* .... $ 12.00
By Jeffrey Little and Lucien Rhodes

Book # 3   *Guide To Investing* .... $ 20.00
By Michael Steinberg

Book #4   *Beyond the Basics: How To Invest Your Money,*
Now That You Know A Thing Or Two .... $ 25.00
By Mary Farrell

Book #5   *Charles Schwab's Guide To Financial Independence* .... $ 12.00
By Charles Schwab

Book #6   *The Intelligent Investor* .... $ 30.00
By Dr. Benjamin Graham

STOCKS

Book #7   *One Up On Wall Street* .... $ 14.00
By Peter Lynch with John Rothchild

Book #8   *How To Buy Stocks* .... $ 16.00
By Louis Engel and Henry Hecht

Book # 9   *Buying Stocks Without A Broker* .... $ 18.00
By Charles Carlson

Book #10   *The New Money Masters* .... $ 16.00
By John Train

BONDS

Book #11   *The Bond Book* .... $ 23.00
By Annette Thau

MUTUAL FUNDS

Book #12   *Bogle On Mutual Funds* .... $ 17.00
By John Bogle

RESIDENTIAL REAL ESTATE

Book #13   *100 Questions Every First Time Home Buyer
Should Ask* .... $ 17.00
By Ilyce Glink

Book #14   *The 106 Common Mistakes Homebuyers Make* .... $ 15.00
By Dr. Gary Eldred

TAX SHELTERED INVESTING

Book #15   *Getting Started In Tax-Savvy Investing* .... $ 19.00
By Andrew Westhem and Don Korn

Book #16   *The New Life Insurance Investment Advisor* .... $ 30.00
By Ben Baldwin

Book #17   *Getting Started In Annuities* .... $ 20.00
By Gordon Williamson

UNDERSTANDING THE ECONOMIC NEWS

Book #18   *The Atlas Of Economic Indicators* .... $ 16.00
\By W. Stansbury Carnes and Stephen Slifer

Book #19   *From Here To Economy* .... $ 14.00
By Tod Buccholtz

Book #20   *How To Read The Financial Pages* .... $ 7.00
By Peter Passell

Book #21   *A Beginners Guide To The World Economy* .... $ 10.00
By Randy Epping

CHILD'S COLLEGE INVESMENT PLAN

Book #22   *The Totally Awesome Money Book For Kids
And Their Parents* .... $ 13.00
By Adriene Berg and Arthur Berg Bochner

INVESTMENT CLUB BOOK

Book #23   *Starting and Running a Profitable Investment Club* ..... $ 15.00
By Thomas O'Hara and Kenneth Janke, Sr.

INDEX INVESTING

Book #24   *Index Your Way To Investment Success* .... $ 16.00
By Walter Good and Roy Hermansen

PERSONAL FINANCE BOOKSTORE ORDER FORM

BY PHONE: CALL TOLL FREE 1-866-799-9901

VISA, MASTERCARD ACCEPTED

BY MAIL: Make check or money order payable to:

PERSONAL FINANCE BOOKSTORE

MAIL CHECK OR MONEY ORDER TO:

PERSONAL FINANCE BOOKSTORE

P.O. Box 55130

Riverside, California 92517

ONLINE: www.personalfinancebookstore.com

PLEASE SEND ME THE FOLLOWING BOOKS. I UNDERSTAND THAT I CAN RETURN THEM AT ANY TIME, FOR A FULL REFUND, IF NOT SATISFIED.

BOOK (#)	QUANTITY	TITLE	PRICE EACH		TOTAL
_____	_____	_____	$ _____	=	$ _____
_____	_____	_____	$ _____	=	$ _____
_____	_____	_____	$ _____	=	$ _____
_____	_____	_____	$ _____	=	$ _____
_____	_____	_____	$ _____	=	$ _____
_____	_____	_____	$ _____	=	$ _____
_____	_____	_____	$ _____	=	$ _____
_____	_____	_____	$ _____	=	$ _____
_____	_____	_____	$ _____	=	$ _____

Book Price Total = $ _____

California Residents Only: Add 8% Sales Tax on Book Total   **Sales Tax =** $ _____

U.S. Shipping and Handling Costs:

$ 4.00 For First Book   **Shipping and**

By Air: $ 2.00 For Each Additional Book   **Handling Cost =** $ _____

ADD BOOK COST TOTAL (+) SALES TAX (+) SHIPPING CHARGES

TOTAL = $ _____

SHIP TO: NAME: _____

ADDRESS: _____

CITY: _____

STATE: _____ ZIP CODE: _____

TELEPHONE # (IN CASE OF ANY QUESTIONS)

(_____) _____ - _____

For inquiries on author availability for interviews/speaking/seminars, etc., call 1-866-799-9902.